Governing Public Organizations

Politics, Structures, and Institutional Design

D0141354

The Brooks/Cole Series in Public Administration

Governing Public Organizations

Politics, Structures, and Institutional Design

Karen M. Hult
Pomona College

Charles Walcott
Virginia Polytechnic Institute and State University

Brooks/Cole Publishing Company
Pacific Grove, California

Brooks/Cole Publishing Company
A Division of Wadsworth, Inc.

Printed in the United States of America

10   9   8   7   6   5   4   3   2   1

Library of Congress Cataloging in Publication Data
Hult, Karen Marie.
   Governing public organizations : politics, structure, and
institutional design / Karen M. Hult, Charles Walcott.
      p. cm.
   Bibliography: p.
   Includes index.
   ISBN 0-534-11592-6:
      1. Public administration. 2. Organization. 3. Organizational
behavior. I. Walcott, Charles Eliot [date]–. II. Title.
JF1411.H86   1989
350–dc19   89-31288
                                                                   CIP

Sponsoring Editor: Cynthia C. Stormer
Editorial Assistant: Mary Ann Zuzow
Production Editors: Phyllis Larimore and Linda Loba
Interior Design: Phyllis Larimore
Cover Design: Sharon L. Kinghan
Manuscript Editor: John Bergez
Permissions Editor: Carline Haga
Printing and Binding: Malloy Lithographing, Inc.

To our parents:
Rita and Robert Hult,
Mary and Arthur Gardner

Preface

This book grew out of lengthy, sometimes fractious conversations about how to think about and account for dynamics and outcomes in organizations as diverse as the U.S. Department of Housing and Urban Development and the NCAA. We kept returning to organization theory. Yet, for all its diversity, the field left us with twin frustrations. First, the inner workings of the organizations we examined seemed to be profoundly political. But many discussions of organization theory exclude politics or treat it as largely irrelevant or, far worse in our view, as pathological. Second, even when a concept of politics is included, it fails to capture all that we as political scientists mean by "politics," which goes far beyond the gaming and maneuvering emphasized by many scholars.

In our view, organizations are inherently political. We find politics whenever groups of people pursue joint action; if that action continues over time, organizations result. Decisions begin to be made in patterned ways, and politics becomes structured. Thus, the study of organizations and the study of politics seem to us to be inextricably bound.

We decided to build on these ideas, exploring how organizations do and should govern themselves. The metaphor underlying our understanding of organizations is that of the political system. In this book, we focus mostly on what we call organizational governance structures and emphasize how these structures influence and are influenced by political dynamics in organizations. Our primary concern is the role of structure in organizational decision making. We take a "problem contingency approach," arguing both that governance structures should (and on occasion do) reflect organizational decision settings and that structures shape participants' perceptions of the problems organizations confront.

These insights produce a series of empirical hypotheses about the emergence of particular governance structures as well as prescriptions for the design and redesign of structures. Among our more important conclusions is that hierarchy, perhaps the most familiar governance structure, is often ill-suited to the sorts of problems that government organizations routinely face. Not only does an emphasis on organizational governance point to possible avenues for structural redesign, it also helps explain why hierarchy is so prevalent.

Our analysis is intended to speak both to readers interested in organization theory and to those interested in public policy. As we suggest in Chapter 1, this book represents a merging of the two fields, exploring the possibilities and challenges of "organization policy." As organization theory, the analysis concentrates on public organizations, where we see an enduring tension between the desirability of hierarchical forms for attaining political accountability and the utility of alternative structures for achieving more effective organizational governance. As public policy analysis, the book argues that organizational forms and processes are proper and necessary foci for discussions of policy making, implementation, and evaluation. We introduce a set of analytical tools and advance prescriptions and criteria for evaluating decision structures and dynamics.

Despite the fact that we are mostly concerned with governance structures and organizational decision making, conceiving of organizations as political systems also suggests a different way of thinking about organizational members — as citizens. From this perspective, people become far more than cogs in an organizational machine; they also have a range of rights and responsibilities. Thus, we also intend this book to be a contribution to the growing literature concerned with such issues as organizational democracy; it will supply, we hope, some institutional building blocks to inform and support an array of philosophical and sociological claims.

As we pursued these ideas, we received considerable help from many colleagues. William Gormley, Elaine Lange, Nancy Lind, Kenneth Mackenzie, Daniel Mazmanian, and Vera Vogelsang-Coombs made useful contributions as we developed our ideas. Lee McDonald and Mary Dietz gave us the benefit of their understanding of citizenship, setting the foundations for our speculations about organizational citizenship. Several reviewers read the entire manuscript and offered numerous suggestions and helpful criticisms: Don Chisholm, Ohio State University; Harold Gortner, George Mason University; Daniel Martin, University of Baltimore; Robert Miewald, University of Nebraska, Lincoln; Joseph A. Pika, University of Delaware; Dennis Riley, University of Wisconsin, Stevens Point; A. B. Villanueva, Western Illinois University; and Gary Wamsley, Virginia Polytechnical Institute. Although errors of fact and logic are ultimately our responsibility, there are now far fewer than there otherwise would have been.

Our students in organization theory, public administration, and public policy analysis at Pomona College, the University of Minnesota, and Hamline University continually challenged us to elaborate upon and clarify our ideas. They also pushed us to apply our model to concrete cases.

Leo Wiegman, our editor at Dorsey Press, was everything we could have hoped for in an editor—encouraging, patient, straightforward, and highly skilled at soliciting constructive and critical reviews. We greatly appreciated the serious regard that Leo, David Follmer, Roger Davidson, and others at Dorsey had for social science writing and for authors.

Our thanks go, too, to the fine people we have worked with at Brooks/Cole. Cindy Stormer greatly eased our transition to a new publisher; we appreciated her competence and enthusiasm. John Bergez sharpened and clarified our prose, while Phyllis Larimore shepherded the book through the production process smoothly and with remarkable dispatch.

Finally, we are grateful for the support and encouragement of our families, friends, and, especially, our parents, to whom this book is dedicated.

Karen M. Hult
Charles Walcott

Contents

The Real World of Organizations

Governance Networks

Tables

Governing Public Organizations

Politics, Structures, and Institutional Design

CHAPTER ONE

Organizations and Organization Policy

On the morning of January 28, 1986, schoolchildren around the country watched as, after repeated delays, the space shuttle *Challenger* finally lifted off. Seventy-three seconds later, *Challenger*, carrying teacher Christa Mc-Auliffe and six astronauts, disappeared in a raging fireball.

The Rogers Commission, appointed by President Reagan to investigate the disaster, moved swiftly. By early June, when it issued its report (U.S. Presidential Commission on the Space Shuttle *Challenger* Accident, 1986; hereafter cited as Rogers Commission), most experts concurred that the immediate cause of the explosion was physical: two O-rings designed to seal together joints on *Challenger's* right booster rocket failed. Pressures from gases inside the solid rocket booster caused it to expand. As it did, its segments rotated against each other. Initially, a temporary seal formed; the heat in the booster melted the O-rings and the putty surrounding them. The seal broke as the shuttle accelerated, releasing a stream of hot gases that ignited an external liquid-fuel tank. The result: the flash and falling debris viewers saw replayed again and again on television.

CHALLENGER: A CASE STUDY IN ORGANIZATIONAL STRUCTURE AND PROCESSES

The more fundamental cause of the accident, however, was *organizational.* The Rogers Commission called the decision-making system for the shuttle program "clearly flawed" (1986, ch. 5). Indeed, the *Challenger* episode is a dramatic illustration of the issues that concern us in this book and of the importance of an accurate understanding of the functioning of organizations.

The Decision to Launch *Challenger*

Myriad factors combined to produce the fateful decision to launch *Challenger*. To begin with, communication problems abounded; several pieces of critical information that might have led to the scrubbing of the flight never reached top decision makers. No one informed key officials of the National Aeronautics and Space Administration (NASA)—Jesse Moore, head of the shuttle program; Arnold Aldrich, manager of the shuttle system; or Robert Sieck, director of flight operations—that fifteen engineers from Morton-Thiokol, the firm that manufactured the booster rocket, opposed the launch, fearing O-ring problems in the unusually cold Florida weather. Indeed, only after the fact did decision makers learn that the temperature at lift-off was 13 degrees below that at the time of any previous flight. Even more startling, the three NASA officials apparently did not know that the primary O-ring had first failed on the second shuttle flight, in 1981. By the end of 1985, O-rings had failed in ten of twenty-three flights. Waivers permitting shuttles to fly on the backup, secondary O-ring had been issued on the six flights immediately preceding *Challenger* (Trento & Trento, 1987, pp. 205, 276). According to the Rogers Commission, NASA officials in Washington were unaware of all of this (1986, p. 84).

How could such information not have been relayed? Part of the reason was extreme competition among NASA's field centers: the Marshall Space Flight Center in Huntsville, Alabama; the Johnson Space Center near Houston; and the Kennedy Space Center in Florida. Especially as the NASA budget grew leaner in the 1980s, the three jockeyed for resources and responsibilities and resisted sharing information or dividing and coordinating tasks. Marshall, where most of the blame for the *Challenger* disaster has been placed, seems particularly turf-conscious. According to space historian John Logsdon, Marshall has "an unusual arrogance, and at the same time a paranoia, perhaps because it has been a place that the Office of Management and Budget wanted to close" (*Los Angeles Times*, 8 June 1986; cf. Romzek & Dubnick, 1987, p. 233). The result, maintained the Rogers Commission, was "a propensity of management at Marshall to contain potentially serious problems and to attempt to resolve them internally rather than communicate them forward" (1986, p. 104). The space center had information concerning problems with the O-rings but failed to pass it on.

Meanwhile, NASA officials in Washington exercised less and less control over the shuttle program. By the late 1970s, headquarters staff had come to rely more on bureaucratic reporting mechanisms instead of the active, "hands-on" monitoring of space center activities characteristic of the agency's earlier days (Romzek & Dubnick, 1987, p. 232). This growing emphasis on mechanistic reporting rather than interaction among professionals restricted communication within NASA. Nor were the bureaucratic requirements carefully followed or enforced: "Paperwork was so neglected by the time the shuttle was flying it was nearly impossible to establish a clear line of responsibility" (Trento & Trento, 1987, p. 183).

At the same time, headquarters officials were preoccupied with mending fences with a budget-conscious Congress and White House, which in turn were being inundated with complaints from commercial and military clients about the shuttle's undependable flight schedule (see, e.g., Romzek & Dubnick, 1987; Trento & Trento, 1987). To make matters worse, NASA Administrator James Beggs was forced to take a leave of absence to respond to a criminal indictment. (The charges were unrelated to the space agency but perhaps were initiated by a hostile White House staff; they were later dropped. See New York Times, 1987; Trento & Trento, 1987, pp. 263ff.) Beggs and NASA staff alike considered Acting Administrator William Graham unqualified.

Yet, to conclude that rivalries and parochialism within NASA were responsible for the decision to launch Challenger is too simplistic. The choice itself was complex and ambiguous. As we have already noted, agency officials faced intense and growing pressures from impatient citizens, public officials, satellite customers, and the media. Moreover, NASA's goals had grown more complicated and uncertain as it entered the 1980s. Its mission extended beyond furthering human exploration of the universe to becoming a "trucking company in space." The agency's criteria for evaluating decision options accordingly broadened from an overwhelming emphasis on *safety* to keeping flights on schedule and maintaining NASA's image of reliability and expertise in order to preserve its long-standing autonomy from Congressional oversight and protect increasingly tenuous funding.

Finally, the decision to launch Challenger was fraught with technical uncertainty and controversy. No matter how compelling the evidence seems in retrospect, at the time of the launch there were no systematic data on the impact of weather on O-ring reliability. According to one source within NASA, debate swirled around "'extrapolations from the same numbers'" (Los Angeles Times, 21 February 1986). Nor was it clear how much risk was being taken in continuing to fly the shuttle despite concerns about the O-rings. "Neither NASA nor Morton-Thiokol fully understood the mechanism by which the joint sealing action [by the O-rings] took place. [They] accepted escalating risk apparently because they 'got away with it last time'" (Rogers Commission, 1986, p. 148). As sharp a critic of the decision process as Caltech physicist Richard Feynman noted that estimates of the likelihood of a shuttle failure ranged from one in 100,000 to one in 100 (Los Angeles Times, 11 June 1986). Even had there been consensus on the degree of risk, few agreed on just how much risk was "acceptable."

Multiple and conflicting goals evidently combined with technological controversy and uncertainty in a setting of high external pressure on NASA to shape the decision rules that most directly influenced the decision to launch. While experts disagreed and top management faced ridicule and censure for continued delays, officials at Marshall had to act. As the Rogers Commission somberly pointed out, these officials shifted the burden of proof to Morton-Thiokol engineers, requiring that the latter demonstrate that "it was not safe to launch, rather than proving it was safe" (1986, p. 118). Morton-Thiokol, heavily dependent on NASA contracts, asked its top technical staff to take off their "engineering hats" and put on "management hats" (Roger Boisjoly, in Rogers Commission, 1986, p. 93). Overriding expert advice, the managers okayed the launch.

What Can We Learn from the *Challenger* Disaster?

The devastating outcome of the decision to launch *Challenger* on that cold January morning dramatically illustrates our dominant theme: organization matters.[1] Far from being the dry stuff of organization charts and procedures for routing memos, organizational factors—formal and informal structures, prevailing norms and values, the distribution and dynamics of power—may not only reflect but also shape the ways in which institutions perceive (or fail to recognize) policy problems, set goals (or wander rudderless), discover and review (or ignore) decision options, and make (or avoid) decisions.

In addition, even the brief reconstruction of the *Challenger* explosion, a spectacularly costly choice, highlights many of the issues that *all* organizations confront. For example:

- How should organizational goals be reconciled with the often narrower concerns of individuals, groups, and subunits within the organization and with the demands of those outside?
- How should an organization ensure that its activities are coordinated and that decisions are based on all available information?
- How should an organization proceed when its goals are ambiguous or in conflict? How should it go about prioritizing goals or making acceptable tradeoffs?
- How should organizations make decisions when there is uncertainty about, or conflict over, cause-and-effect relationships (that is, over the means to particular ends)?[2]

Underlying these questions is a key premise: that there is a relationship between the *form* of decision making and the nature of the decision *outcomes*. Certainly, NASA's decision structures shaped the ways in which key officials perceived the decision to launch *Challenger*. A different set of

---

1 Scholars have engaged in lengthy discussions about the meaning of "organization" (see the reviews in, e.g., Gortner, Mahler, & Nicholson, 1987; Harmon & Mayer, 1986). Most generally, organizations can be conceived as entities that gather people together to pursue joint action over time. Following Herbert Simon (1976), we treat organizations primarily as decision-making systems.

2 The first two questions are similar to the three that Herbert Kaufman (1964) poses in his essay "Organization Theory and Political Theory."

decision-making structures might have produced a different launch decision and perhaps even called into question the existence and goals of the entire space shuttle program.

If one rejects the view that organizations are merely products of their environments (as, we shall see, many "natural systems theorists" believe), then a crucial question for organizational analysts and policy makers alike becomes: what forms of decision making are most appropriate under given circumstances? Such a question in turn underscores the need for what we will call (following Landau, 1983) *organization policy*. Organization policies provide guidelines for designing and redesigning organizations in ways that are most appropriate to the pursuit of their missions. Useful organization policy increases the probability that decision making will contribute to, rather than block or hinder, the attainment of desired policy outcomes.

Exploring appropriate modes of decision making sets inquiry on a path that leads one to consider not only organizations but all human collectivities. As Herbert Kaufman argued in the early 1960s, political theorists have wrestled with such issues at least since the time of Plato and Aristotle (cf. H. Wilson, 1975). Although the words of political philosophers may have a more explicitly normative ring than those of many contemporary organization theorists, the concerns are much the same: the meaning and purpose of community and the *polis*; the role and direction of governing bodies, and who determines them; the obligations and rights of participants in collectivities (their "citizens").

VIEWING ORGANIZATIONS AS POLITIES

These are the issues and values that ground the consideration of organizations we undertake in this book. The commonality of concern among political philosophers, constitution writers, and students of organizations underscores the fact that many of the questions that both analysts and members of organizations confront are fundamentally *political*. That is, they have to do with making choices, allocating benefits and burdens, generating commitment and legitimacy, and coping with conflict, complexity, and uncertainty. This in turn suggests that one approach to understanding organizations is to conceive of them as political systems, or *polities*, that develop structures for channeling political dynamics and performing political tasks.

Contributions of the Polity Approach

This viewpoint represents a relatively unusual way of thinking about organizations and about organizational politics. In contrast, much of the literature in both organization theory and public administration treats organizations not as polities but as either *control systems* or *natural systems*.

From the control system perspective, organizations are tools for attaining agreed-upon ends. At least in aspiration, organizations are relatively stable entities that seek to minimize or reduce unpredictability and to solve discrete problems. Control emerges as an important focus of attention (cf. Landau & Stout, 1979; Stout, 1980): to what extent, and how, do organizations achieve control over internal activities and external demands? Since organizational goals and interests are taken largely as givens, authority rather naturally flows from the top of an organization down (though it may not in all actual cases). Organizations thus tend to rely on hierarchical authority and decision structures: hierarchy is consistent with stability and with the joint pursuit of shared objectives. Control analysts acknowledge that organizations sometimes confront turbulent environments and uncertainty over appropriate goals or technologies. But in the control system view, an organization does not seek to incorporate ambiguity or value diversity into its decision structures as much as it strives to control and minimize them.

Uncertainty and controversy are more central to the natural system understanding of organizations. Indeed, from this perspective, organizations can do relatively little to control ambiguity and conflict, which emanate from their environments. Organizations respond to, but cannot always shape, these driving forces outside their boundaries. Because environments vary, organizational structures also will be diverse, extending beyond the fairly simple hierarchies often emphasized by control theorists. Such structural variation largely reflects environmental dictates rather than organizational innovation or experimentation. Like biological organisms, organizations evolve in an effort to better adapt to environmental forces. The measure of success becomes survival.

Politics, as we have defined it, fits rather awkwardly with either of these understandings of organizations. Some who hold the control system view argue that politics is pathological, to be reduced or eliminated whenever it rears its ugly head. Mayes and Allen (1977), for example, define politics as any organizationally "unsanctioned" activity, and Mintzberg (1983) calls it "illegitimate." Other control theorists don't go this far, instead identifying politics with group or individual pursuit of self-interest, which may or may not be congruent with organizational interests (e.g., Allen et al., 1979; Gray & Ariss, 1985; L. Porter, Allen, & Angle, 1983; Zaleznik, 1970). Yet, even when authors suggest that politics might benefit organizations, they hedge their bets. Politics may provoke problem-solving responses as organizations seek to increase control over those with possibly "deviant" goals. In other cases, politics may facilitate the organization's adaptation to demands for change as subgroups become advocates for external interests. But often politics simply appears to be annoying or irrelevant. It reduces to "office" or "jungle" politics, fun or distasteful to observe or play, but essentially unrelated to the primary focus of attention—the pursuit of organizational goals.

Organizational politics is not much more important for those viewing organizations from the natural system perspective. They recognize that internal politics may ease or impede the organization's responsiveness to the environment. Still, the primary factors for understanding organizational actions and dynamics remain outside.

The "organization as polity" perspective flows from very different notions. It begins with an understanding of politics as an organizational-level phenomenon: organizations themselves are political rather than serving only as arenas for the playing out of the self-interested "micro-politics" so often scorned by control system theorists (cf. Connolly, Conlon, & Deutsch, 1980; Evan, 1976). Certainly, competition among individuals and groups takes place, but the polity perspective contends that organizations develop structures to channel these dynamics, much as nation-states rely upon elections, hearings before legislative committees, and administrative rule making.

Organizations perform a range of other political tasks as well. They often must search for and set goals, not simply select the most appropriate response (or even an "adequate" one) to given ends. As in national political systems, goals—the "public interest"—are likely to be diffuse and negotiable. Public agencies, for example, frequently are charged with multiple, vague, and competing objectives. The Environmental Protection Agency (EPA) must balance its mandate to preserve and enhance the nation's air, water, and land, and to protect public health, with demands that individuals be able to travel how and where they wish and that economic interests be protected. Organizations also must often employ ambiguous or controversial policy technologies and face myriad constituents, clients, competitors, and overseers. The "best available control technology" required by the EPA does not always produce desired declines in pollution, and the agency's efforts to determine the health effects of particular substances or the impact of given policies on economic development have proven notoriously difficult. Meanwhile, members of Congress, environmental and industry groups, local public officials, and citizens press their views.

In coping with such uncertainty, controversy, and complexity, organizations must do more than make decisions and manage conflict. They must also allocate costs and benefits, and they must seek to foster among their members and constituencies a sense of the legitimacy of and a commitment to the collective enterprise. Yet, even in the face of such demanding environments, the polity perspective holds open the possibility that organizations can actively shape, not merely respond to, their environments.

Performing political tasks may well require that organizations develop a range of structures in addition to the authoritarian hierarchies emphasized by an understanding of organizations as control systems. Especially as ambiguity and controversy mount, the *processes* by which goals and means are selected, challenged, implemented, and revised may become key. Legitimacy in and out of an organization may derive largely from the manner in which decisions are made rather than from the content of the decisions themselves. As we shall see, many kinds of structures can be observed in contemporary public agencies—for example, interagency task forces, citizen advisory committees, administrative adjudication, informal rule-making procedures, and technical review panels. Among the recommendations of the Rogers Commission were the inclusion of astronauts in NASA's management decisions and the creation of a safety advisory panel of outside scientific experts. Most such "reforms" are defended not only because they may yield substantively "better" decisions but also because they satisfy important "process values" (Mashaw, 1985) such as representativeness and accountability. Nor can structural diversity be fully explained by looking at environmental forces, as the natural system view seems to suggest. Citizen advisory panels, for example, pervade government and are used by agencies with quite different missions in a range of very different environments.

In short, whether observers view organizations as control systems, natural systems, or political systems has significant implications for the questions they ask, the ways they search for answers, and the prescriptions they propose. We believe that politically informed approaches—those that focus on organizations as polities—deserve more attention. Students of organization theory and public administration increasingly concur on at least one point: organizations and managers alike must learn to cope with uncertainties and conflicts rather than seek discrete solutions to readily identified problems. Under these conditions, politics as we have defined it assumes center stage. As many are beginning to suggest (e.g., Gawthrop, 1984; J. O'Toole, 1985), a self-aware, consciously designed process of change—in which organization policy plays a key role—can help organizations handle even pervasive ambiguity and controversy. Only rarely, we will argue later, will this activity entail sole or even primary reliance on hierarchy. A perspective that views organizations as polities may thus hold special promise, for it directs attention to a broader variety of structures and norms for channeling organizational dynamics than most views of organizations as control systems can accommodate. At the same time, the political system view holds open the possibility that organizations can be much more than reactive creatures of their environments.

The Governance Model

Questions about the nature and possibilities of organization policy lie at the core of politically informed approaches to organizations. Much remains to be learned. As pivotal as decision structures may be to organizational dynamics and outcomes, the issue of which sorts of structures are most appropriate for what kinds of settings remains largely unexplored.

We will examine these issues by concentrating on a single politically informed approach, which we call the *governance model*. It provides one way of synthesizing and assessing ideas from the literatures of organization theory and public administration, a language for thinking about organizations, and an alternative means of addressing the issues raised by the Rogers Commission and by human collectivities generally.

The governance model focuses on *political structuring* in organizations. Because it flows from a view of organizations as polities, the model posits uncertainty and controversy, generated both inside and outside of organizations. It also assumes that organizations actively seek to cope with these circumstances: they take what measures they can to reduce uncertainty and to keep controversy within manageable bounds, leading ultimately to an organizationally acceptable decision. In addition, the governance model anticipates that an organization's approaches to handling problems involving uncertainty or controversy become more standardized as the problems recur. The resulting decision-making routines are what we will call *governance structures*. For any class or type of decision, these structures specify who is entitled or required to participate, how the participants may interact, and what constitutes a decision.

Because the settings in which organizations operate and decisions are made vary so widely, one would expect many different kinds of structures for organizational governance to develop. This observation leads us to two of the questions taken up in the following chapters. First, what is the range of possible structures, and what general types can be identified? Second, how is the type of governance structure related to the setting within which it operates? The latter question opens up a host of empirical and normative issues. What factors account for the occurrence of certain structures? Given a set of circumstances, can we recommend a particular kind of structure?

The insights of the governance model are of special relevance for public organizations. Not only do government agencies frequently confront decision settings characterized by ambiguity, controversy, and complexity, but the "political" character of public administration has been widely recognized (Downs, 1967; Rourke, 1984; Seidman & Gilmour, 1986). Meanwhile, the search for improved governmental performance and heightened responsiveness—a search that may be furthered by redesigning governance structures—continues.

While our emphasis will be on public organizations (primarily, but not exclusively, government agencies), we intend the governance model to be a useful intellectual tool for considering *any* organization. Indeed, recent works in management theory (e.g., J. O'Toole, 1985; Pfeffer, 1981) have begun to discuss similar notions with reference to private organizations, although they have not integrated their ideas with prevailing views of organizations.

The governance model by no means taps all of the insights generated by an understanding of organizations as political systems. The polity perspective points, for example, to the significance of the less structured interplay among individuals and groups in organizations. Such politicking is the foundation for what chapter 2 will call the "political arena model," which highlights internal struggles for power and domination. Thinking about organizations as political systems also might lead one to consider the meaning and nature of "citizenship" in organizations and to examine the rights and obligations of organizational members (which we will be able to do only briefly). In contrast, the governance model concentrates on decision-making structures within and between organizations. Such an emphasis is compatible with concerns about micro-level politicking and organizational citizenship, for governance structures likely shape and reflect both. Still, it must be recognized that we highlight only part of what is "political" in organizations. More than either the political arena model or concerns with organizational citizenship, governance analysis sees organizations as striving for internal and external legitimacy as they struggle to make decisions in the face of uncertain and controversial policy goals and technologies.

Nor does the governance model address all that is implied by discussions of the management of complex organizations. We understand "management" to encompass both "governance" and "control." As we will elaborate, governance issues mainly concern decisions (and non-decisions) about overall organizational missions, major activities, rights to participate in decision making, and general relations with the environment. Some of the concerns of control theorists are less significant for this model—for example, the details of supervising employees, monitoring their performance, and coordinating work flows. Although these matters of administration and control are crucial in organizational life, to the extent that they provoke little uncertainty or controversy, they are less relevant politically. Consideration of organizational governance instead directs attention to the search for values and goals and the development of the broader strategies that together shape administrative tasks.

WHAT FOLLOWS

In what follows, we elaborate on the issues of organizational politics and structural redesign, exploring the potential and the limitations of organization policy. Chapter 2 explicates more fully the contrast between the understanding of organizations as polities and the control system and natural system perspectives and provides the details of the governance model. This discussion both suggests the distinctiveness of the governance model and delineates the questions explored in the rest of the book.

At the foundation of the governance model and of organization policy is the assumption that governance structures should (and on occasion do) vary according to the problem settings in which they are embedded. The following four chapters pursue the implications of this premise.

Chapter 3 spotlights the analytical anchor of the governance model—the structuring of organizational polities. The chapter discusses various explanations for the emergence and persistence of organizational structure, justifies its significance within the governance framework, and provides a sense of the enormous variety of possible governance structures.

Chapter 4 shifts attention to the decision settings confronted by organizations. It emphasizes the varying degrees of uncertainty and controversy over policy goals and the means of achieving them, and it examines the numerous sources of uncertainty and controversy inside and outside of organizations.

Chapter 5 links these notions to structure, outlining a "problem contingency" approach to organizational design. After laying out criteria for appropriate structuring, it sketches an argument for which governance structures seem most appropriate for given decision settings. The chapter also briefly explores some of the effects of particular structural choices.

Although actual organizational structures sometimes mirror the prescriptions of the governance model, frequently they do not. Hierarchical structures seem to dominate, even though the goal consensus and technical certainty to which they appear best suited often elude policy makers. Chapter 6 examines the reasons for seeming mismatches between structure and problem setting, and seeks to account for the prevalence of hierarchy.

Of course, many decisions channel through more than one governance structure, emerging from the interplay of several structures and their routines for search, consideration, and ratification. In the public sphere, analysts often examine entire policy arenas and their associated "iron triangles" or "issue networks," which join actors across branches and levels of government and between the public and private sectors. Chapter 7 considers how structures mesh within and across organizations to form a variety of *governance networks*. It also seeks to discover which networks are most appropriate for particular decision settings.

Chapter 8 returns to the level of the organization as a whole. It considers how governance structures and networks might intertwine to produce distinct organizational political systems, with implications for the distribution of power in organizations and for the values they tend to pursue. In addition, the discussion examines the implications of organizational political systems for their members, or "citizens," and explores the many meanings and challenges associated with the notion of organizational citizenship.

Weaving through our exploration of organizational governance are the concerns of organization policy. To what extent, and how, we will persistently ask, can public institutions be designed to attain the purposes that the larger society expects them to serve? These questions inexorably take us beyond dry explications of structure as either an "independent" or "dependent" variable to considerations of the distribution and dynamics of power within and between organizations, and of broader external forces as both potential shapers and possible mirrors of organizational structures and activities. They also raise fundamental issues about the appropriate place of organizations in the contemporary United States and about the implications of organizations for their members, clients, constituents, and overseers, as well as for the society as a whole.

Chapter 9 draws these themes together, reflecting upon the opportunities for systematic organization policy, as well as its limitations. As a conception of organizations as polities should already lead one to expect, no easy answers emerge. However, at least tentative paths for structural redesign can be charted.

This sensitivity to the opportunities for and the tensions generated by organizational design may be the most important contribution of the governance model, one that is especially compelling as we move beyond the 200th anniversary of the U.S. Constitution. It brings public agencies under the same umbrella of normative concerns about decision structures that animated the founders as they struggled to construct and justify the rest of the governmental system. Those who view organizations primarily as control systems emphasize improving the efficiency, effectiveness, and productivity of governmental agencies. Their partisans can be found among students of public administration and advocates of governmental reorganization. The aims of these "reformers" (Salamon, 1981) are not wrong, we believe, but rather too limited. When goals are in dispute and policy technologies are unknown or unreliable, when constituents cry for responsiveness and clients demand "humane" treatment, agency competence cannot be the sole criterion for assessing government organizations or prescribing reforms. Instead, lessons drawn from the framers may still be apt: tradeoffs among competing values must be made and remade as situations change; institutions can facilitate or inhibit this process; structural variation and experimentation are likely to be necessary. As NASA officials may realize in the aftermath of *Challenger*, structures that performed adequately in certain settings may sabotage organizational efforts as circumstances change. Yet organizations need not be captives of their environments: structural redesign may improve an organization's capacity to cope with evolving conditions.

All this implies that we will be concerned throughout this book with the intellectual issues that confront both organization theorists and public policy analysts. Conventional classifications of the social science literature typically place organization theory and public policy analysis in separate categories. The potential for linking the two has long seemed clear, and scholars, especially those in the field of public administration, certainly have recognized it (see, e.g., Gortner, Mahler, & Nicholson, 1987; Harmon & Mayer, 1986). However, the nature of the relationship between organizational design and policy making remains elusive and the academic subdivisions largely distinct (cf. Meltsner & Bellavita, 1983).

To us, this seems much more than an academic issue. Organizational problems in NASA evidently were at the root of the *Challenger* disaster. In a similar vein, John Chubb (1988) contends that organizational redesign may hold the key to improving elementary and secondary education. Schools organized into participatory teams of faculty and administrators significantly outperform those with hierarchical relations between teachers and principals. Most current reforms, he argues, fall short by not treating schools as complex organizations, with rules and norms of behavior, responding to a range of environmental forces (Chubb, 1988, p. 29).

The premise that structures may shape policy outcomes animates our concern with organization policy. We seek to understand the relationship between structure (as defined by the governance model) and the making and implementation of policy. Our ultimate objective is to use that understanding as the basis for prescribing organizational means that heighten the likelihood of attaining desired policy ends. Although agreeing upon those ends will always be difficult, and achieving them can never be guaranteed, we believe that organizational design can enhance government's capacity to produce "good" public policy.

CHAPTER TWO

Metaphors and Models of Organizations

Over a century ago, John G. Saxe (1882) wrote a poem recounting the Hindu fable of the Blind Men and the Elephant. Six blind men, the story goes, encountered an elephant. Each touched a different part of the beast and so reached a different conclusion about what an elephant is really like. For instance,

> The first approached the Elephant,
>   And happening to fall
> Against his broad and sturdy side,
>   At once began to bawl:
> "God bless me! but the Elephant
>   Is very like a wall!"

Encountered sidelong, an elephant is indeed like a wall. But different angles reveal other aspects of the beast. The blind man grasping the tail, for example, decided the elephant resembled a rope; the one who encountered the elephant's leg knew for certain that an elephant is like a tree. The poet concludes:

> And so these men of Indostan
>   Disputed loud and long,
> Each in his own opinion
>   Exceeding stiff and strong.
> Though each was partly in the right
>   And all were in the wrong!

Dwight Waldo, an organization theorist, has compared the efforts of his colleagues in this field to those of the fabled blind men (1961, 1978).

There are many theories of organization, but each lays hold of a different aspect of the beast, and no one of them can be regarded as definitive.

Waldo's analogy expresses an important truth: *what* we think about organizations reflects *how* we think about them. Organizations, like most social phenomena, are incredibly complex. More than that, they are largely intangible. The "real" elements of organizations may have physical manifestations, but their essence is hard to find and even harder to measure or gauge accurately. Organizational purposes, for instance, can be written down in mission statements or on "culture cards" (see, e.g., Whiteside, 1986, p. 85). Yet what is written is rarely identical to what actually guides organizational members.

MODELS AND METAPHORS IN
ORGANIZATION THEORY

In order to better understand organizations, analysts construct simplified models to represent complex realities (see, e.g., Hoover, 1988; Kaplan, 1963; Nachmias & Nachmias, 1987). A model contains what the modeler believes to be the most important "characteristics of some empirical phenomenon, including its components and the relationships of the components" (Nachmias & Nachmias, 1987, p. 47; see, e.g., Allison, 1971).

Modelers begin with a set of rules for determining which elements of what they are modeling are important enough to warrant inclusion. Ideally, theory supplies the criteria. Yet, organizational scholars (with the possible exception of rational choice theorists, such as Bendor, Taylor, & Van Gaalen, 1987; Hammond & Miller, 1985; and Miller & Moe, 1983) have not come very close to developing theories that can be expressed as simply, elegantly, and powerfully as most theories in the natural sciences. Lacking such theory, organizational analysts turn to the next-best thing for guidance when they simplify: they look to metaphors of organization.

A metaphor is an image or a figure of speech in which a particular object or idea is used in place of another, thus suggesting a similarity between them. Using metaphors seems to be a helpful way for scholars to get a handle on a complex reality that available theory neither fully describes nor elegantly explains (cf. Ortony, 1980; Stone, 1988). More generally, metaphors can be "central to the task of accounting for our perspectives on the world: how we think about things, make sense of reality, and set the problems we later try to solve" (Schon, 1980, p. 254; cf. Landau, 1972, ch. 3). In the 1960s, those concerned with arresting the deterioration of central cities characterized slums as "congenital diseases" and "natural communities" (Schon, 1980, pp. 262–68). The finest poetry shows the remarkable capacity for insight and illumination that this kind of thinking can have. On the other hand, examples abound to demonstrate the limits and dangers of metaphorical thinking; for instance, nations may overreact in times of conflict if their leaders have long thought of their enemies as "devils" whose regimes are "evil empires."

Metaphors pervade the literature of organization theory. A recent work (G. Morgan, 1986) identifies eight such images that express the thoughts of theorists or critics of organizations. In this chapter, we will summarize three organizational metaphors. We discuss two of them—the organization as control system and the organization as natural system—because they have been the most influential in shaping current schools of organizational thought. We examine the third, which views organizations as political systems, because it lays the basis for the central argument of this book. We then explore that argument, expressed through a model of organizations as systems of governance.

Throughout our discussion, we will be at pains to point to the limitations as well as the advantages of any particular metaphor. Despite their common invocation of the idea of a "system" (that is, a whole comprising functionally interconnected parts), the three images that we will discuss portray organizations in significantly different ways. They are partial truths, like the conclusions of the blind men about the elephant. They allow us to see some aspects of organizations clearly, but at the same time they obscure others. All can be helpful approximations or dangerous stereotypes. All are, almost by definition, simultaneously "true." But, we will contend, they are not always equally useful in helping one describe organizations, account for their dynamics and outcomes, and offer prescriptions.

Organizations as Control Systems

When two or more people wish to accomplish a common task, they often divide up the work, each taking care of a different part of it. This strategy requires some coordination—it may even be necessary to appoint somebody to do that job—but it allows people to specialize, doing a similar task repeatedly rather than moving from one kind of activity to another. In this way, people may become more efficient, producing more work for less effort.

The strategy of dividing labor, described by Adam Smith in 1776, lays the foundation for organizations. If a task is to be repeated, the people involved typically will find it advantageous to divide the labor in the same way as the first time, taking advantage of the experience each person has gained in a particular part of the job. When this procedure is repeated often enough, creating the expectation that the job will be broken up again in the same way in the future, the formal structures of division of labor and supervision associated with organization emerge. Viewed in this light, an organization is a consciously designed instrument, a rational tool for attaining the purposes of its creators. Its principal objective is to achieve maximum predictability of actions and products—that is, control over its subparts—in order to maximize efficiency in production.

Organizations, in other words, may be viewed as *control systems*. Striving for predictability is perhaps the most basic and obvious feature of organizations. Thus, the earliest organizational thinkers in the late nineteenth and early twentieth centuries considered organizations to be devices for attaining efficiency through control. These scholars took for granted that the organizers and leaders of organizations understood their goals clearly and had developed (or could easily discover) appropriate technical means for reaching them. The *organizational* questions that remained involved two problems: first, how to select and manage individual workers so as to maximize their productivity; and second, how to design the relationships among those workers—thus creating the "formal organization"—so as to attain optimum efficiency in the utilization of labor.

By the early 1900s, a loosely knit group of scholars and practitioners, now commonly referred to as "classical" management theorists (see, e.g., Shafritz & Ott, 1987), began to address these matters systematically. Individuals identified with the "scientific management" school of thought (see, e.g., Merkle, 1980) focused primarily on the first issue. Foremost among them was Frederick Winslow Taylor, whose book *Principles of Scientific Management* (1911) was a landmark in the study of organizations. Taylor and his colleagues advocated "scientifically" selecting workers and designing jobs.

Once jobs were designed and workers chosen, the problems of motivating the employees and supervising their work came to the fore. Although interested in motivation, the scientific managers paid very little attention to individual psychology. Rather, they simply assumed that workers were rational economic actors—that is, that they worked only to make money and would do whatever they could to make the most money possible. Taylor recommended a piece rate system, in which workers' pay was determined by their output. Since, he argued, a piece rate would mean that maximizing production was in the interest of workers and managers alike, increased productivity would doubtlessly occur.

These assumptions were challenged in the now-famous series of studies carried on in the late 1920s and early 1930s at the Hawthorne (Illinois) plant of the Western Electric Company. This research revealed some of the psychological and sociological complexity of the workplace. Contrary to the "rational economic actor" view, individuals appeared to be motivated as much by recognition and security as by money. Moreover, work groups had their own stable, "informal organizations," in which leadership did not depend upon the official positions of authority in the formal hierarchy. Taylor's simple models of employee selection and motivation did not account for what was observed in this research.

Organization theorists and managers still did not question scientific management's fundamental orientation toward control, however. Rather, they looked for ways to extend managers' control over workers in light of these new findings. Thus was born the "human relations" school of management, which stressed the development of leadership and the motivation of employees through noneconomic incentives. Its effect was to update Taylor's theories and tactics, but not to question his purposes (see Perrow, 1986, ch. 3).

The second major issue of organizational control concerned how to design organization *structure* to permit optimal control of people and organizational processes—again, with the objective of attaining maximum efficiency. Many classical theorists are best remembered for their discussions of the principles by which organizations should be designed (see, e.g., Gulick & Urwick, 1937). These principles included such basic and still-familiar design principles as the scalar chain (authority should run from top to bottom in a hierarchy), span of control (superiors should not supervise too many subordinates), specialization, and unity of command (each worker should report to one superior). Classical management thinkers argued that the proper application of these principles—which required some judgment, since they were general and sometimes even contradictory (cf. Simon, 1946)—would result in an organization that ran as efficiently as possible. Nothing in these writings suggested a need to view government agencies differently from private firms. The image of an efficient machine seemed entirely appropriate for both.

Probably the most influential thinker on structural design, however, was German sociologist Max Weber (1946), who concentrated on "bureaucracy," with special emphasis on the public sector.[1] Unlike his American and European counterparts, Weber was not interested in advising managers on how to make organizations more efficient. Indeed, he feared the consequences of bureaucratic efficiency for democratic government. But Weber did outline the fundamental characteristics of what he called *bureaucracies*, and his analysis in many ways resembles those of other classical thinkers, especially in its stress upon formal, consciously designed relationships and procedures. Weber identified such properties as hierarchy, the prevalence of general rules, and exclusive reliance upon officials who were chosen for their competence and who pursued their jobs as careers and often were given tenure for life. All this ideally would serve to ensure that public officials would be both competent and nonpartisan; hence, they would make fair and entirely predictable decisions.

Thus, both Weber and other theorists of organizations as control systems saw the principal thrust of organizing as creating predictability, stability, routine, and order—in short, as permitting the exercise, from the top, of thoroughgoing control over all the elements of the organization. The people in the organization were simply cogs in a machine, perhaps a bit less reliable than the other parts, but needing to be rendered as reliable as

---

1 Weber (1946) was published posthumously in 1922, but not translated into English until after World War II.

possible so that the machine as a whole could realize its potential. Gareth Morgan (1986, p. 33) succinctly expressed these thinkers' assumptions about the aims of management: "plan, organize, and control, control, control."

It is hard to overstate the impact of this metaphor of the well-run machine. The control system image has become the basis for most people's perceptions of organizations, and it has had a continuing influence upon the theory and practice of management (see the emphasis placed upon it by, e.g., Abrahamsson, 1977; Bolman & Deal, 1984; Dow, 1988). In American public administration, the metaphor has underlain the recommendations of virtually all the task forces and study commissions that have sought to restructure and redirect the federal executive branch, invariably in the name of "efficiency" (e.g., the Brownlow Commission and the Hoover Commissions). Moreover, it has provided important ideological support for the essentially authoritarian structures of modern public and private management (cf. Morgan, 1986; Pfeffer, 1981).

Nevertheless, like all metaphors, the control system perspective is not a fully adequate portrayal of organizational reality. It is limited in several important ways. First, much of the thinking that has been done within this framework virtually ignores human psychology, advancing an overly simple theory of worker motivation. From the tradition of Taylor, we have the assumption that people are maximizers of economic benefits, period. Human relationists see more complexity, but they still tend to argue that *all* people respond mostly to nontangible, socioemotional factors. Second, the control system metaphor encourages us to pay little attention to the environments within which organizations function, assuming that the rest of the world is stable and predictable (cf. Bolman & Deal, 1984, p. 57). In this view, organizations are largely self-reliant, "closed systems" (Katz & Kahn, 1978; J. Thompson, 1967, pp. 4–6). Third, the metaphor takes organizational goals and the technical means of attaining them as givens, or at least as problems for which solutions exist that can be objectively discovered.

Each of these omissions and assumptions helps to give the image of organizations as control systems the virtue of sustaining a focus on certain key elements of organizations: they *do* involve many relationships of control. At the same time, this image entails ignoring some crucial aspects of organizational reality.

Organizations as Natural Systems

The insights that led to the development of the human relations approach to management had implications beyond the initial rush to develop new techniques for controlling employee behavior in the interest of the organization. As Gareth Morgan puts it, a "new theory of organization began to emerge, built on the idea that individuals and groups, like biological organisms, operate most effectively only when their needs are satisfied" (1986, p. 41). Theorists began to speculate that organizations had more "organic" than "mechanistic" features (e.g., T. Burns & Stalker, 1961). Discussions of organization theory began to assert an alternative metaphor: the image of organizations as natural (living) systems.

The full flowering of this biological metaphor came when scholars began to suggest that entire organizations, not just the people and groups within them, had the characteristics of natural systems. This perspective was inspired by members of several disciplines who labeled themselves "general systems theorists." Perhaps the most significant work was that of Ludwig von Bertalanffy (1968). His general systems theory posited that all natural phenomena, from atoms to ecosystems, share the same broad properties and can be subjected to the same basic kind of analysis. Of the many insights generated by this approach, the most important for organization theory was that natural systems exist within a broader environment; if they are to survive in that environment, they must adapt to it.

Looking beyond organizational boundaries highlighted the richness, diversity, and importance of the environments within which organizations must function. Organizations in this view are open rather than closed systems (e.g., Katz & Kahn, 1978); environments supply organizations with resources, impose sanctions and constraints, and provide feedback on their performance. The dependence of private firms upon suppliers and customers is obvious; somewhat less apparent but equally significant are the ways in which firms are affected by legal regulation, technological change, general economic conditions, and a host of other factors. Similarly, in public agencies, the surrounding environment of clients, legislative committees, interest groups, the press, and the public has an important impact on policy making and implementation as well as on budgetary allocations.

Once the importance of the environment was underscored, the task for natural systems theorists was to systematically trace its impacts. *Survival* became for the natural systems metaphor what efficiency had been for the view of organizations as control systems: the dominant goal and final measure of success. For natural system thinkers, adaptation implied flexibility in several dimensions. They believed organizations could adjust—sometimes intentionally, at other times by chance—such characteristics as the nature and relationships of their subsystems, their productive technologies, and even their goals in order to pursue the imperative of survival. In effect, organizations came to be treated largely, though not entirely, as products of their environments (cf. Abrahamsson, 1977; Van de Ven, 1983, p. 44). For example, researchers argued that optimal structural form was contingent upon the nature of the environment (e.g., T. Burns & Stalker, 1961). In a turbulent, unstable environment, more "organic" (decentralized, flexible) arrangements best promoted survival, at least among private firms. In calmer settings, "mechanistic" organizations with preprogrammed responses to environmental demands became more appropriate. Where different subunits interacted with different environments, subunit structures might diverge greatly (e.g., Lawrence & Lorsch, 1967).

It is somewhat harder to fit the natural system image to public agencies, primarily because the survival of public agencies is problematic far less often than that of organizations in the private sector (Kaufman, 1976). Still, scholars of public organizations have become acutely sensitive to the web of relationships that links an agency to its surroundings and that clearly affects the agency's purposes and behavior. Agencies may not fear total demise, but the absence of that fear does not prevent them from competing, expanding, and practicing what Matthew Holden called "imperialism" (Holden, 1966; cf. Downs, 1967). In effect, the argument that agencies seek mainly to grow and prosper—rather than, for instance, to carry out their legislative mandates most efficiently and effectively—is identical to the general claim of the natural systems perspective that organizations' ostensible goals should not be taken literally (cf. Katz & Kahn, 1978, pp. 18–20). In the face of environmental threat or opportunity, formal goals are negotiable in a way that the more fundamental imperative of survival is not. In this sense, the organization viewed as a natural system is the antithesis of the rational tool assumed by the control system perspective.

The natural systems metaphor calls our attention to some fundamental aspects of organization that are neglected by the image of organizations as control systems. The focus upon environments is clearly important. Not only do environments shape organizational goals, structures, and activities, but especially in the public sector most would insist that external influence (particularly from Congress, the executive branch, and the public) *should* guide agency action. Important, too, is the stress on organizational adaptability and innovation; especially as the world grows more turbulent, organizations need to be able to change more quickly than the view of organizations as control systems seems to allow. This suggests in turn that the hierarchical arrangements emphasized by many control system theorists will only rarely be appropriate. Similarly, the contention of natural systems theorists that organizations respond to their own imperatives rather than to the ostensible purposes of their founders or their proclaimed goals conveys a necessary insight.

On the other hand, the natural systems perspective has its own problems and limitations. Gareth Morgan (1986) points out two major ones. First, comparison to biological systems—the most common analogy—conveys a notion of organizations that is too concrete. As we insisted at the outset, organizations are mostly intangible; moreover, unlike biological organisms, they need not die or inexorably deteriorate with age. Second, the ideas of functional interrelatedness and "harmony" stressed by the natural systems metaphor overstate the degree of integration that we actually find in organizations. Such notions may even promote a misguided ideology that insists upon too much integration of individual personalities into organizational systems. Members of organizations from IBM to the Walt Disney Company to the U.S. military sometimes complain that their employers go too far in promoting uniformity by insisting on similar physical appearance, demeanor, and values.

Beyond these problems lies a larger one. Just as the control system metaphor assumed efficiency to be the overriding goal of organizations and their managers, the natural system view looks to survival, or some near equivalent. In neither case is the question of goals, directions, or purposes for the organization seen as a problem that might have more than one solution. In each perspective, there is a "true" objective, although it might sometimes be obscured by misleading assertions about goals. A picture of highly integrated organizations, virtually imbued with lives of their own, whose main features tend to be imposed upon them by their environments, seems to minimize the relevance of human purpose. Yet the reality of organizations, as we observe them, is shot through with the often un-harmonized behavior of humans and their sometimes competing or ambiguous purposes.

This may be the most serious limitation of the natural systems metaphor. It is especially difficult to accept such an image in analyzing public organizations, since the political theory that animates government presumes that goals, and the process of goal setting, are of crucial importance. An understanding of organizations as political systems, to which we now turn, seeks to address the shortcomings of the control and natural systems metaphors.

Organizations as Political Systems

For a very long time in the history of organization theory, discussions of power and politics were almost taboo. The prevailing emphasis on control left little room for "politics," a term that connoted conflict and disagreement, if not sheer self-seeking. In a properly run organization, most scholars concurred, there would be little or nothing to disagree about, and mechanisms of hierarchical authority would handle any problems. As for "power," it resided only in hierarchical authority. The introduction of the natural systems metaphor did little to change this neglect. This view tended to treat conflict as a failure of integration or of organizational or personal adjustment, and therefore as a symptom of ill health. When natural system thinkers discussed conflict at all, they usually concentrated on how to manage or control it.

Nevertheless, anyone with experience in an organization could tell often lurid stories of "politics." Typically, the term was reserved for individuals seeking to enhance their personal standing, or that of their units, through such devices as gossip, flattery, and secretive maneuverings. This sort of "micro-politics" was deemed generally unfortunate by orthodox scholars and managers, though it came to have its defenders as a common and occasionally valuable element of organizational life (cf. Mintzberg, 1983). Moreover, as people who have tended to be disadvantaged in organizations—especially women and minorities—became conscious of their plight and determined to change it, the claims they made and the issues they raised were expressed in the language of political debate (cf. Kanter, 1977). Women and minorities sought increased entry to and influence in organizations both by protesting and building coalitions within organizations and by pressing for external intervention through court decisions, affirmative action laws, and the like. In this kind of activity, politics becomes a means for raising legitimate questions that organizations must strive to answer.

Casting fundamental organizational issues in political terms forces one to consider a more comprehensive idea of politics. Our notion of politics places it at the center of how organizations discover, articulate, and pursue their basic purposes and the means to achieving them (cf. Mason, 1982, p. 13). Even to discuss such matters requires that we accept the idea that ends and means are not always settled issues. Invoking the idea of efficiency does not solve the problem, since people can agree to be efficient but still differ over what they are trying to be efficient at doing or how it may be most efficiently done. Likewise, the guiding star of survival is not sufficient to navigate by, for there are usually many routes to survival, leaving real choices to be made about which to take. Moreover, it is nearly inevitable that well-meaning, reasonable people will sometimes disagree over these issues and will try to ensure that their views prevail. As a result, we are drawn to see politics as a necessary aspect of organizational life.

These points make a credible case for politics as something to be found in all organizations, but how does this recognition constitute a distinctive way of understanding organizations? The beginnings of such thinking may be found in the work of the scholars of the "Carnegie school" (see especially Cyert & March, 1963; March & Simon, 1958), who pointed out that, in practice, organizations' stated goals are often ambiguous or vague. As a result, organizational subunits must define for themselves "operational" goals that can be rendered concrete enough to pursue. However, these operational goals are not always in harmony with one another, a fact that may lead to conflict among subunits. For example, the overall goal of the Defense Department is to provide military security for the country. But this shared goal does not stop the Army, Navy, Air Force, and Marines from disagreeing frequently over priorities and concrete objectives. Controversy also may arise over the appropriate means for attaining even agreed-upon ends (cf. J. Thompson, 1967). Determining how best to discourage international terrorism—even when an acceptable definition of "terrorism" can be reached—provokes ongoing debate among the State and Defense departments, the FBI, the CIA, and the White House staff.

Organizational directions and the means for proceeding, if they are to be harmonized at all—and sometimes they are not (Cyert & March, 1963)—

must be dealt with by dialogue, debate, or a process such as coalition formation. This latter notion, with its corollary that victory will go to the strongest coalition, has been elaborated by a number of scholars (e.g., Bacharach & Lawler, 1980; Pettigrew, 1973; Pfeffer, 1981).

Raising the problems of determining goals and selecting means implies a host of related issues, such as participation rights (who is permitted to affect the decision?) and legitimacy (how are all concerned persuaded to accept the outcome?). Introducing these considerations makes it clear that we are developing an image of the organization as something much more than a control system or a natural system. In this view, the organization becomes a political system, or polity.

A polity is a political community; the term is derived from *polis*, the ancient Greek word for city-state. Polity refers both to institutions of government and to the social and cultural milieu in which they are embedded. The Greeks had a high regard for governance—a notion that evokes images of guiding or steering the "ship of state"—and for politics, the processes through which governing takes place. Without appropriate political institutions, and appropriate education of citizens in their use, none of the other benefits of civilized group life—culture, industry, even self-defense—could be realized fully. Politics served both to allocate values (the benefits and costs of membership in political society) and to generate purpose and commitment, to give meaning to the society.

Organizations can be viewed in an analogous fashion. Organizations have mechanisms for governing themselves, whether these mechanisms are collective bodies, like the Legislative Strategy Group in the Reagan White House, or the power of final approval of departmental regulations, such as that exercised by the Secretary of Health and Human Services. Similarly, organizational members often share an ideology, or set of values about how power is to be allocated and exercised and how decisions are to be made (see, e.g., Hoover, 1987, pp. 4–5; Shafritz, 1988, p. 271). This common ideology, which is part of an organization's "culture" (e.g., Schein, 1985), also may indicate what sorts of ends and means are appropriate. Unless attention is paid to governance, the potential benefits of organization, including efficiency, may well be incapable of realization. Viewing organizations as polities highlights the challenges of governance and the fundamental role of politics in organizational life.

MODELS OF THE ORGANIZATION AS A POLITICAL SYSTEM

The image of a polity or political system is a very general one. There are many different ways to understand politics; thus, many possible models may be derived from the insight that organizations are political systems.

We will look in some detail at two of these. The first, which we will call the model of the organization as a "political arena," is important because it captures both a commonplace attitude toward politics on the part of organization members and the public and an interesting movement in contemporary organization theory. We will advance the second, a model of organizational "governance," as an alternative to the first.

The Organization as a Political Arena

The model of the organization as a political arena is built upon the assumption that organizational goals and the means for achieving them are the outcomes of intraorganizational competition. "Organizations [are] 'alive and screaming' political arenas that house a complex variety of individuals and interest groups" (Bolman & Deal, 1984, p. 109). This understanding has been raised to the level of a model most explicitly by Jeffrey Pfeffer (1981), whose "political power model" portrays organizations as controlled by "shifting coalitions and interest groups" participating in a "disorderly" decision process; the dominant ideology views the organization as a forum for "struggle, conflict, winners and losers" (Pfeffer, 1981, p. 31). Pfeffer sees this sort of competition as sporadic, often unpredictable, purely self-interested, and largely unbound by generally understood rules and conventions.

In the political arena model, the primary analytical task is to explain how the winners win and why the losers lose. The most general answers are cast in terms of "power." But to avoid falling prey to tautology (since winners are always more powerful in some way or another), analysts have had to specify the various kinds and uses of power within organizations. Thus, scholars have devoted attention to the manipulation of factors like information, symbols (cf. Pfeffer, 1981, ch. 6), technology (cf. Crozier, 1964), informal networks and alliances, and various strategies for coping with the external environment (cf. Pfeffer & Salancik, 1978; for a comprehensive treatment, see the essays in Allen & Porter, 1983). Empirical investigations of organizational politics then offer explanations of the outcomes of particular organizational struggles in terms of such power resources (see, e.g., Allison, 1971, chs. 5, 6; Halperin, 1974).

The resulting literature of anecdotes and case studies makes it very clear that those who employ the model of the organization as a political arena are on to something real and important. As Gareth Morgan (1986) notes, the analyses also help us to explode the myths propounded by the other schools of thought that we have examined. For example, the political arena model directly challenges the notion that organizations always are, or ought to be, "rational" and "efficient" and directs attention to the basic question of whose interests are served by particular organizational decisions. Similarly, the orientation toward politics is a useful corrective to the natural system assumption that organizations naturally tend toward harmony and integration.

On the other hand, treating organizations as political arenas is not a final answer, either. Morgan (1986, p. 198) warns that looking at the organizational world through this lens leads to a tendency to emphasize "the cynical, selfish, ruthless, get-ahead-at-all-costs mentality" and that practical advice based upon such an understanding may tend to turn its listeners into what Michael Maccoby (1976) called Jungle Fighters (cf. Hale, 1988). Beyond that, we may wonder whether all organizations really do reflect a plurality of interests; perhaps instead the *expectation* of pluralism obscures larger truths, such as a fundamental class cleavage between management and labor or, conversely, a genuine harmony of interests (cf. Bolman & Deal, 1984).

Our main criticism of the model of organizations as political arenas is related, but a bit different. As we have noted, this model leads one to look for actors seeking to advance their interests by amassing the elements of power. The basic mechanism for promoting one's cause is the relatively unstructured power struggle. In effect, such a model seeks to characterize entire organizations by looking at relatively small-scale, or micro-phenomena that occur episodically within them.

This emphasis has two major weaknesses. First, the model does not readily lead to interesting theory. What it does produce is inventories of the elements of power, which in turn yield analyses that purport to show how certain interests prevailed over others thanks to better resources or superior strategy (see Heymann's parallel discussion of studies of "bureaucratic politics," 1987, p. xiii). Such a model permits only *ad hoc* analysis of individual cases. This can lead to useful (or, sometimes, misguided) advice, but it does not generate much overall theoretical insight into organizations, since typically little emerges that is generalizable across organizations or decision settings (cf. Bolman & Deal, 1984, p. 217).

The second limitation is best expressed in terms of common sense. A view of organizations as combat zones may be consistent with reports of the atmosphere in the worst sorts of firms and government agencies, but it is not congruent with what we know about most such institutions, most of the time. The notion that organizational leaders would permit, or that members would long tolerate, such a series of free-for-alls seems unrealistic. In most human institutions, where conflict of interest and purpose is bound to happen sometimes, efforts are made to contain such events. This is not to say that conflict is always suppressed. Rather, rules emerge to govern the conduct of the competitors, and formal channels for handling conflict and its resolution develop in order to render fair verdicts and to limit the duration and extent of altercations. In effect, politics becomes institutionalized, subject to routines like most other organizational activities.

To the extent that the model of the organization as a political arena misses this reality,[2] it presents an overstated and ultimately misleading picture of organizations and of organizational politics. In the next section, we will introduce a model of organizational politics that draws heavily upon the insights of the model of the political arena but seeks to go beyond it in describing how politics is really handled in most organized settings.

The Governance Model

The term *governance* flows from the notion of an ordered polity. Ideally, the net effect of politics in a constitutional order is not disruption but collective decision making that is authoritative and legitimate. When governing is done well, according to agreed-upon procedures, participants may accept the outcomes of political competition without resorting to coercion, since they concede the legitimacy of the system itself and thus are prepared to acquiesce in its consequences. In applying this logic to organizations, we adopt the term *governance* to refer to politics that is conducted within relatively structured settings, bound for the most part by rules. The rules may be formal, prescribing that conflicts be settled in particular forums by certain people, or they may be informal understandings among the participants. The structures may be specialized instruments for handling political matters, or they may be used for other tasks, such as control and supervision.

In subsequent chapters, we will detail the forms, or structures, that organizational governance might take. For now, though, we can simply refer to the example introduced in chapter 1. Prior to the launch of *Challenger*, NASA found itself in a matrix of competing goals and pressures. The agency's sense of its mission included considerations of both efficiency and safety: the former argued for on-time launches, the latter, often, for delay. The overall goal was ambiguous. Moreover, technical questions, such as the likely effect of cold weather, had to be factored in. In these complex circumstances, how was the decision to launch the space shuttle reached? The answer is more complicated than a simple hierarchical model of organizational decision making or an emphasis on internal politicking provides. The decision was made according to an interlocking series of processes that required the input and acquiescence of a number of people and that permitted outside influence—for example, that of subcontractors and of the president's staff—to affect the outcome. This was no improvised power struggle, but a recurring cycle of decision making and influence,

2 A partial exception is Jeffrey Pfeffer (1981), who does discuss institutionalizing power and politics. Even so, he focuses primarily on strategies and tactics, with structure serving mainly as a power resource or constraint. Moreover, Pfeffer evidently believes that politics remains outside of, and may be expected to be disruptive to, the anticipated and desired rhythms of organizational life. "Rationality," he notes, "will be difficult to restore" once politics breaks out (1981, p. 32). Thus, control lurks behind the scenes as a desired outcome and ultimate objective.

some of it formally prescribed by agency procedures, some informally added on in practice. Decision making, in short, was shaped by intertwined structures for organizational governance.

The governance model of organizational dynamics, like the other views we have discussed, provides only a partial understanding of organizational reality. We do not claim that all organizations have fully developed systems of governance or that governance systems are always successful in channeling the political life of the organization constructively or satisfactorily. But we do suggest that the phenomena of governance, in one form or another, are important aspects of all organizations.

Assumptions about politics. As we noted earlier, a governance model makes assumptions about the nature of politics that are different from those that are usually found in organization theory. When discussing these contrasting views of politics in organizations, we cannot avoid facing up to the basic definitional question: what do we mean by "politics"?

Certain properties are common to all understandings of politics. Political issues arise when people must live or act jointly and must therefore pool their efforts and their ideas. More specifically, we suggest, opportunities for political interaction occur when members of a group face the need to make choices together in the face of uncertainty or disagreement. The case of disagreement, normally expressed in some form of conflict, is well understood by all students of politics, who agree that politics is a form of conflict resolution, a way of ironing out disagreements without having to resort to physical force. In order to function this way, the institutions of political decision making must command enough respect that even those whose wishes do not prevail will choose to accept a decision rather than forcibly resist it. We refer to that capacity to gain acceptance as an institution's "legitimacy," perhaps the key objective of organizations understood as governance systems.

But politics is about more than conflict. Sometimes individuals and groups face not controversy but uncertainty: they may be genuinely in doubt about their values and objectives, or unsure of the consequences of action or inaction. Uncertainty may revolve around relatively small, technical matters, such as how best to ensure the safety of a space shuttle, or around very large issues of collective goals, such as the objectives of the U.S. space program. A political process may thus be one in which a group acts, not to resolve disagreement, but to reduce uncertainty—for instance, by pooling information or brainstorming about the likely consequences of possible actions—thereby permitting choices to be made, and ends and means to be selected.

Both uncertainty and controversy are present in organizations at many times and in many forms, as chapter 4 will elaborate. Not all organizations face political choices routinely or continuously, however, though some surely do. The Bureau of Weights and Measures confronts uncertainty or controversy only very occasionally. The president's White House staff deals in them practically all the time. Certainly, though, it would be hard to discover a government agency of any type that never becomes involved in politics as we have defined it.

Those familiar with the traditions of American public administration scholarship and practice will note immediately that this approach to politics explicitly rejects the conventional distinction between "politics" and "administration." This idea, advanced by Woodrow Wilson (1887), holds that, ideally, "political" decisions are made by elected officials. The role of public agencies should simply be to carry out those mandates, an activity that need not involve public administrators in making political choices. A more modern version of the argument concedes that top political appointees of government agencies cannot avoid politics but holds that career civil servants must do so. This attitude is clearly expressed in the avowed purpose of the American civil service: to provide "neutral competence" for the operation of the government.

Our position on this matter coincides with that of the administrative "realists," who have been pointing out persistently at least since the end of World War II (e.g., Appleby, 1949; Stein, 1952; cf. Hale, 1988, p. 428) that, whatever the theory may hold, administrators do make political decisions, because they have no other choice. Our example of the *Challenger* disaster is simply one instance of a situation of this kind. To be fair to Wilson and his heirs, what they really were claiming was that administrators must avoid being partisans, or advocates of a particular agenda or ideology. In other words, their definition of politics was considerably narrower than the one we employ. Thus, we are not really taking issue with them: we do not particularly advocate administrative partisanship. But we do insist that much of what bureaucrats do, much of what agencies and departments do, must be viewed as political in order to be fully understood.

Politics in this sense encompasses far more than bureaucratic scheming for tactical advantage in struggles over power and turf. We are interested in what Philip Heymann calls the "politics of management," which involves "guiding an organization constructively and creatively over years in a world of powerful political forces" (1987, p. xiii). The governance model emphasizes the ways in which structures—recurring patterns of organizational behavior (discussed more fully in chapter 3)—facilitate and inhibit an organization's capacity to cope with uncertainty and controversy.

Governance analysis, then, focuses on more than "bureaucratic politics" (examined splendidly by, for example, Allison, 1971; Downs, 1967; and Halperin, 1974). It also diverges from conventional investigations of "administration." These latter studies, relying on at least an implicit understanding of organizations as control systems, emphasize the ways in which organizational structures perform control functions such as coordinating the activities of organizational members and permitting superiors to direct and evaluate performance. The notion of governance, in contrast, seeks to capture the dynamics of an organization's search for the orienting values and goals and the broader policy strategies that set the parameters and provide the direction for its efforts at control.

Questions raised by a governance model. To this point, we have argued that the governance model is worth considering because it identifies and highlights important organizational characteristics. Since all models are partial, however, perhaps the best argument for employing any particular model revolves around its utility. What will members of organizations or students of organization theory find in the model of organizational governance that can be useful to them? We believe the answer is threefold: the model can lead to significant gains in describing, explaining, and prescribing for organizations.

First, the model helps in *description*. We have talked in very general terms about what governance structures do, but we have illustrated only incidentally what they look like, what they "are." A number of descriptive questions remain. How many different kinds of governance structures are there? Are they found only or mostly at the top, or "policy," levels of organizations, or do they occur throughout them? Can any organization be characterized as having a certain kind of governance structure, or do most organizations contain a variety of structural types? Is there a relationship between the policy area an organization is engaged in and its dominant kinds of governance structures? If, as our example of *Challenger* suggests, governance structures are linked to one another in complex "governance networks" that often transcend organizational boundaries, how do these structures mesh, and what kind of overall labels or characterizations can we apply to these networks? All these are questions of identification: we need an exhaustive inventory of governance structures and networks.

More important, perhaps, is the question of what difference governance structures make. Granted that governance, in the sense of the decisions that are actually made, matters, does it matter *how* these choices are made? Will the substitution of one structure or set of structures for another change organizational outcomes in predictable ways? Is organizational governance, in other words, something that the designers or managers of organizations can and should manipulate?

Description of structural forms and their consequences is useful, but inadequate if it simply stops there. As social scientists, we will want to go farther, trying to *explain* both the occurrence of governance structures and their consequences.

An important set of questions involves how and why these routines for the handling of political choice do or do not develop. Under what circumstances are the authoritarian governance arrangements that accompany classical hierarchy—that is, when the boss makes the decisions—inadequate? How do organizations or their leaders recognize this inadequacy? How is the apparent tension between nonauthoritarian governance and the hierarchical structures of control reconciled? Does it even need to be reconciled? Under what conditions do particular types of governance arrangements emerge, and what consequences do they have?

We will not be able to give definitive answers to many of these questions in this book. The model of organizational governance is new, and the base of empirical research needed to provide full answers does not yet exist. However, we will outline the issues and provide descriptions and approximate explanations on the basis of what is now known.

As we develop an inventory of governance structures and their interrelationships, along with some tentative notions about the differences they might make, we can begin to offer some practical suggestions. Thus, the governance model also aims at *prescription*. Organization theory often has had a prescriptive intent: in some way, it strives to make organizations better. An understanding of organizational governance should be able to make such a contribution as well. We will need to specify the criteria of desirability, or what constitutes good governance. Then, drawing upon our understanding of the consequences of structural types, we can attempt to show that particular forms are more or less appropriate under various circumstances.

This exploration should move us a bit closer to the development of *organization policy*. By recognizing and analyzing the critical organizational properties highlighted by the governance model, we hope to begin to make it possible to design or redesign organizations with an eye to improving governance.

THE GOVERNANCE MODEL AND PUBLIC ORGANIZATIONS

Historical and critical analyses of bureaucracy have consistently identified a set of problems that seem inherent in formal organizations. One, foreshadowed by Max Weber and elaborated by contemporary critical theorists, is that organizations are oppressive, both of those within and, potentially, of those without. The image presented in these writings is one of organizations as relentless mechanisms of control, inherently dehumanizing in their quest for efficiency (cf. Harmon & Mayer, 1986, ch. 10). Without entering the epistemological debate pursued by interpretive and critical theorists, we can suggest that their understanding of reality perhaps owes too much to the image of organizations as control systems. Seen as a polity, the organization may not seem entirely benign—indeed, many organizational political systems are not—but the potential for human freedom within them appears to be greater. If the notion of efficiency is viewed not as an all-controlling imperative but as itself an often-ambiguous criterion, a new perspective may be obtained.

This perspective not only challenges the predominance of the efficiency criterion but forces us to look beyond hierarchy in our search for structural principles. Hierarchy in some form may be the inevitable consequence of seeking to maximize control over the organizational machine. But it is not necessarily the only way to go about governing a polity. More constructively, there may well be at least a general resemblance between the critical theorists' call for full, authentic communication within organizations and the requirements of several of the forms of governance structure that we will identify in the next chapter.

A related issue was more centrally the subject of Weber's concern and continues to be the focus of modern scholars such as Charles Perrow (1986). It is that bureaucratic organization, precisely because it is the most efficient organizational form and the one that is maximally in command of usable expertise, will tend to dominate the governmental arena, to the detriment—even the imperilment—of democracy. Our analysis suggests an alternative view. To the extent that government organizations are actors within the larger body politic, they will themselves be shot through with the uncertainty and controversy characteristic of political processes. Thus, they will likely be permeated by ambiguity and conflict, since these properties both lie at the root of the processes by which goals are formed and means selected, and are inherent in the techniques of politics. Organizations that would govern the national polity will themselves be polities, as indeed all large organizations must be, to some degree. Seen in this way, government agencies may or may not be a danger to popular government. They do not have to be.

Finally, another persistent criticism of U.S. government agencies is that they are too "political." As we have noted, this argument rests upon an overly narrow conception of politics. While the idea of governance is in principle neutral with regard to administrative partisanship, it is not neutral with respect to politics. Politics is not just necessary and inevitable, it is welcome. We recall the ancients' regard for politics: it is the primary challenge confronting society and the one whose undertaking makes possible the other benefits of collective existence.

Ultimately, a model of organizational governance seeks to describe, explain, and make prescriptions concerning the processes of constitution building for the political entities within which most Americans spend much of their working day. It thus tends to subsume treatments of organizational democracy and to borrow from them a focus upon the rights of individuals in all organized social settings, especially those characterized by a significant degree of potential coercion. Many approaches to organizational governance are possible, just as the range of normative political theories is vast. With that in mind, it is important to note that the ideas advanced in the chapters to follow constitute only one of the possible approaches. Nevertheless, like the concepts of governmental structure available to the framers of the American Constitution, these ideas are building blocks for conceptualizing and designing a diverse array of institutions.

CHAPTER THREE

Governance Structures

The promise that redesigning governmental structures might produce desired outcomes has long preoccupied American thinkers and politicians. The framers of the Constitution hoped that their blueprint for separate institutions sharing power would filter public passions and restrain the overweening ambitions of officeholders, while also producing more effective and authoritative policy than government had generated under the ill-fated Articles of Confederation. Later, John Calhoun sought to dampen the growing conflict among the states through the doctrine of "concurrent majorities." In the late nineteenth and early twentieth centuries, Progressive-era reformers tried to wrest state and local governments out of the hands of corrupt party officials, reorienting government to the pursuit of efficiency and the public interest (see, e.g., Knott & Miller, 1987, ch. 3; Schiesl, 1977). By the 1930s, Franklin Roosevelt moved to conquer the Depression and, later, responded to World War II by creating a vast web of new agencies (cf. Knott & Miller, 1987, ch. 4). In contrast, Presidents Carter and Reagan attempted to demonstrate their activism by promising to streamline and dismantle parts of a "bloated and overgrown" executive branch. As Alexis de Tocqueville observed more than 150 years ago, Americans are inveterate tinkerers with the machinery of government, confident that "human institutions can be shaped at will" (1945, vol. 1, p. 45).

That such optimism is misplaced has been the refrain of social scientists for many years. Scholars (e.g., March & Olsen, 1983; Meier, 1980; Szanton, 1981) find scant evidence that the form of government organization makes much difference or that it can be manipulated to produce desired ends. Indeed, some, like March and Olsen (1983), go so far as to assert that large-scale government reorganization has almost entirely symbolic meaning. It is perhaps the opiate of politicians and citizens alike, inducing the illusion of action to address pressing problems without effecting real change.

Yet not everyone reaches such a dismal conclusion. Other researchers have presented evidence suggesting that organizational redesign *can* influence policy effectiveness and government accountability, and that theoretical understanding of its consequences is possible (see, e.g., Hult, 1987; Maynard-Moody, Stull, & Mitchell, 1986).

Arguments about the effects of reorganization tend to be conducted within the intellectual framework of organizations as control systems and thus tend to revolve around the notion of efficiency. But the positive findings also point to other consequences, including changes in the substance of policy, in the responsiveness of agencies, and even in the overall legitimacy of government activity. Thus, to fully appreciate the impact of changes in structure, we need a broader view than that provided by the control system perspective.

It is at this point that the governance model enters the dialogue. It highlights the nature of institutional structures and their implications for political decision making, and it aims ultimately at offering prescriptions for organizational redesign. Thus, we side with James Madison, Thomas Jefferson, and their intellectual progeny: the governance model assumes that structure can influence organizational activity and performance. At the same time, the model cautions analysts to hedge their bets. For structure also may reflect a diversity of environmental, organizational, and human factors, and its effects are neither guaranteed nor always anticipated.

Before we can fully explore the role of organizational structure, however, the notion of structure itself must be examined more carefully. Then we can contrast governance structures to other conceptualizations and sketch the variety of governance structures that can be found, or could be introduced, in public organizations.

VIEWS OF ORGANIZATIONAL STRUCTURE

The idea of structure pervades most discussions of organizations. Even those who ultimately dismiss its impact often begin with some notion of structure, if only to cast in relief the factors they believe are significant.

The Concept of Structure

Most generally, *structure* refers to *recurring* interactions in organizations.[1] It offers the observer a "snapshot of [a] unit's behavioral processes" (Eulau, 1986, p. 102) and a sense of the rules that underlie these patterns of interaction. Thus, structure encompasses not only hierarchically or legisla-

---

1 For a good overview of organizational structure, see Hall, 1987.

tively sanctioned mechanisms ("formal" structures, such as procedures for memo routing and rule making) but also more informal practices, such as policy breakfasts and discussion groups. Particular structures may grow directly out of formal rules, or they may evolve as more habitual "standard operating procedures." These structures may be relatively permanent or more temporary.

That structure is an inherent feature of organizations is not surprising. Structures respond to the desire for predictability and reliability in collective human endeavor, a key reason for establishing organizations in the first place. Structures offer "agendas" that can facilitate and coordinate individual action by providing information on joint strategies, procedures, aims, and the activities of others (Hammond, 1986). Moreover, structures help impose "boundaries of rationality" that define and delimit tasks and channel information and responsibility. This last function arguably compensates for limited human cognitive capacity and scarce time, energy, and attention (Cohen, March, & Olsen, 1976; March & Simon, 1958; Simon, 1976). As tasks become routinized, one no longer needs to worry about discovering ways to perform them. To the extent that structures become more permanent, or "institutionalized," they contribute to continuity, serving as a "bank or repository for the accumulated competence" of an organization (Bragaw, 1980, p. 248).

Organizational structure also can be seen as a response to internal and external normative imperatives, or ideologies. For example, it establishes "participation rights," determining who has access to which decision arenas (March & Olsen, 1983). Kenneth Boulding conceives of structure as a " 'constitution,' . . . a previously agreed method of resolving conflicts which have not yet arisen" (in Hammond, 1986, p. 402). Such imperatives take on added force in the public sector, for "organizational structures affect the legitimacy of [the larger] political system as well as its governability, representativeness, and rationality" (Olsen, 1983, p. 9). Thus, citizen advisory panels, congressional subcommittees, and clearance of proposed agency regulations by the Office of Management and Budget are examples of structures that were designed in part to keep agencies accountable to the public and to elected officials. This insistence on external monitoring of, and participation in, agency affairs clearly indicates that a "closed system" understanding of government organizations is inappropriate. It suggests, too, that prescriptions for more hierarchy inside public agencies are likely to be misplaced.

Structures and Organizational Systems

This rather expansive view of structure contrasts sharply with what many envision when they hear the term "organizational structure." Conventional treatments in management science, sociology, and public administration focus on structure as a means of realizing such "control" objectives as dividing labor, specifying spans of control, and securing unity of command. More generally, various orientations toward organizations spotlight different aspects of organizational structure. Examining these differences will bring the characteristic concerns of the governance model into sharper focus.

Not surprisingly, the image of organizations as control systems emphasizes the role of structure in enhancing (or inhibiting) an organization's efficiency and problem-solving capabilities. Following the logic of Max Weber (1946), structure becomes primarily a means of dividing labor and of directing and coordinating activities. Well-designed structures "economize on bounded rationality" and thereby improve performance (M. Meyer et al., 1978, p. 150; Simon, 1976). They also clarify power relations, focusing subordinates' attention on organizational goals (M. Meyer et al., 1978, p. 150). Structure, in this view, is predominantly formal and permanent; its purpose is to promote organizational effectiveness and efficiency.

Natural system theorists highlight quite different properties. They see structures as more flexible and subject to change as organizations respond to environmental demands. From this perspective, one may expect a greater variety of structures to emerge, with environmental "selection" of the most appropriate form (Hannan & Freeman, 1977b; Kaufman, 1985). At the same time, organizations may deliberately use structures to absorb environmental turbulence and protect routine work, introducing, for example, legislative liaison offices or ombudspersons to handle external complaints. Structure may help organizations survive in another way: structures sometimes perpetuate convenient "myths" that permit organizations to appear to be following "rational procedures" (J. Meyer & Rowan, 1977). Thus, schools may develop elaborate placement mechanisms for tracking students into classes according to their "abilities," as well as grievance procedures for appealing such assignments. Despite the notorious difficulties of defining and measuring "ability" and the tendency of placement and grievance proceedings to favor white middle- and upper-class students, the structures may help reassure critical outside observers that school officials are pursuing educational quality and procedural fairness (see, e.g., Gortner, Mahler, & Nicholson, 1987, pp. 275–87).

Viewing organizations as political systems yields a third understanding of structure. It underscores the ways in which politics in organizations is channeled, routinized, and legitimized. Although the political arena model pays some attention to such ordering, political structuring lies at the very core of the governance model. *Governance structures* emerge as people in organizations strive to develop patterned ways in which to discover and articulate goals, select among means, cope with uncertainty and controversy generated both within and outside the organization, and foster legitimacy and commitment inside and outside of the organization.

The discussion that follows highlights these structures of organizational governance. It is important to reiterate, however, that, like other treatments of organizations, this one captures only part of the elephant. An emphasis on governance structures highlights the political responsibilities that we believe are a fundamental and inevitable component of organizational management. We shall pay correspondingly less attention to the more control-oriented uses of structure for dividing, coordinating, and supervising work (though, as we shall see, structures may perform both control and governance functions). Similarly, while the governance model acknowledges that the environment influences structure, it does not always accord it primary importance, as do most natural system views.

THE EMERGENCE OF GOVERNANCE STRUCTURES

The governance model treats organizations as *clusters of governance structures*. For example, a unit of professionals (lawyers, say, or economists or toxicologists) may operate by consensus internally, have representatives serving with other subunits or agencies on project teams, and be part of the agency hierarchy responding to orders from top-level officials. Moreover, some professionals in the unit may participate in helping settle employee grievances or meet regularly with colleagues with similar training in other agencies or on legislative staffs. Despite their disparate nature, all these activities are forms of organizational governance, and their repetition creates what we call governance structures.

Governance structures may be activated in a number of ways. Some are in force more or less permanently. Mechanisms for appointing and promoting civil servants, for example, are taken almost for granted. Other structures, such as labor-management negotiations or budget consultations, are routinely activated: in the first instance, by expiring contracts; in the second, by the budget deadlines set by the Office of Management and Budget. Project teams and task forces appear as circumstances warrant— for instance, to assist localities with spills of toxic chemicals. Still other structures may be *ad hoc*, improvised in the face of unanticipated crisis or opportunity. President Kennedy turned to the ExComm (the Executive Committee of the National Security Council) during the Cuban Missile Crisis (Allison, 1971); some state governors convened special advisory teams to recommend ways of responding to the revenue surpluses produced by the 1986 federal tax changes.

The processes by which organizational structures of any kind emerge are not very well understood. The governance model provides one way to begin to explore these dynamics by introducing the notion of *differentiation of governance structures*. "Differentiation," in this context, refers to the creation, formally or informally, of structures primarily for conducting governance (rather than administration—the concern of, e.g., Blau, 1970, and Blau & Schoenherr, 1971).

What fosters such differentiation? In part, as we have suggested, governance issues become more salient as uncertainty or controversy grows within the organization or in the environment (cf. Walcott & Hult, 1987). For example, beleaguered public health agencies currently struggle to respond to the spread of AIDS amid controversy over the seriousness of the situation, disagreement over appropriate government actions, and continuing uncertainty over the exact mechanisms of transmission. In other instances, mounting internal dissatisfaction with present policy strategies or an influx of recently trained professionals into an organization may trigger insistence that different approaches to policy problems be considered. Mechanisms designed for control and administration become less satisfactory under these turbulent conditions, for they treat ends and means as basically unproblematic. Differentiated governance structures—for example, special AIDS task forces with representatives of the scientific, medical, gay, and political communities, or project teams to experiment with new techniques—can help focus organizational attention on making decisions in less settled circumstances.

These structures also may buffer more routine activities from ambiguity or conflict. In many private firms, for instance, bargaining and grievance procedures have evolved, providing forums outside the normal work setting for airing complaints and involving employees in organizational decision making. Federal agencies, sensitive to increasingly watchful courts and suspicious congressional committees, lean more on offices of general counsel (West, 1987) and on advisory panels of outside experts (Rhodes, 1982) and citizens when formulating rules and regulations; these devices may defuse environmental hostility or help filter it into organizational decision making. Given numerous—and, probably, mounting—sources of ambiguity and controversy (detailed in chapter 4), one can expect to find considerable evidence of differentiated governance structures in most public organizations.

In addition, differentiation itself may spawn further differentiation, generating a *differentiation dynamic*. The introduction of differentiated governance structures increases an organization's internal complexity, which may heighten the degree of conflict and uncertainty present within the organization. Increased conflict and uncertainty may, in turn, boost demand for additional governance mechanisms, enhancing diversity and launching a new cycle.[2] For example, the growing threat of government regulation led many private firms to establish units specializing in environmental protection, affirmative action, and consumer affairs (see Scholz, 1984). These new structures were charged with lobbying regulators, interpreting rules and anticipating problems for the rest of the organization, and monitoring the organization's efforts to comply with government regulations. Not surprisingly, such changes introduced "new channels of commu-

2 See a parallel argument linking the multiplication of control structures to the demand for additional supervisory and administrative mechanisms in Blau and Schoenherr (1971, p. 213).

nication and alternative chains of command" (Scholz, 1984, p. 147) and triggered jurisdictional disputes and uncertainty over organizational objectives and strategies. The response: additional governance structures, such as task forces and strategic planning committees, established to try to channel and contain new controversies and ambiguities.

As the differentiation dynamic plays itself out, an organization may devote more and more attention to issues of governance. This need not be a blessing, especially when the organization also is assessed in terms of criteria of control and efficiency. In some cases, too great a preoccupation with governance may hamper performance and slow decision making (Hage, 1980, p. 328; Pasmore, 1986, p. 248).

To discuss differentiated governance structures is not to suggest that such structures perform *only* governance tasks or that undifferentiated structures have no governance functions. Rather, it is a question of emphasis. Differentiated governance structures are *primarily* charged with searching for and legitimizing ways of coping with uncertainty and controversy; they also may perform more control-oriented roles, such as assigning tasks to various workers and coordinating activities. Similarly, undifferentiated structures do more than divide labor and provide for the supervision and evaluation of employees; they also shape and reflect organizational choices about how ends and means will be selected and benefits and costs allocated.

Simple hierarchy is probably the most familiar undifferentiated structure; primarily designed for control, it also performs governance tasks. In hierarchies, information flows from subordinates to superiors; directives, rewards, and sanctions flow in the reverse direction. Lines of authority and decision procedures typically are well specified (in principle, if not in practice). Although hierarchies focus more attention on control than on governance, their implications for organizational politics and governance are clear. In a hierarchy, ambiguity and conflict likely will be difficult to channel into decision making, for they will not necessarily be recognized or treated as significant by established routines for monitoring the environment and internal affairs. Instead, they are apt to be explained away (e.g., Lange, 1988). Moreover, hierarchies prescribe a particular pattern of influence and authority, one that is stratified according to formal position.

Thus, in the governance model, all structures—differentiated and undifferentiated, formal and informal—contribute to our understanding of how organizations govern themselves. By examining structures, we can gain insight into how organizations are likely to choose ends and means and how they can be expected to respond to internal and external change. Further, structures do more than shape ongoing governance; they also reflect past political dynamics. Structures provide a glimpse of how previous issues were resolved (or quasi-resolved); they suggest, too, what directions were set, which participants were included (and which excluded), and what distribution of benefits and burdens resulted.

THE VARIETY OF GOVERNANCE STRUCTURES

To this point, our discussion has only hinted at the many types of governance structures that organizations may rely upon. Certainly, the range of structures extends beyond the hierarchy emphasized by those who view organizations as control systems. Although there are few inventories of possible structures, numerous theorists have proposed, and many practitioners have experimented with, what we would call governance structures.

Often, such structures are designed to supplement and enhance the operation of existing control mechanisms. Procedures for labor-management negotiation or expression of employee grievances, for instance, may smooth routine work. Missouri has introduced over 125 "quality circles" in state government. In these circles, groups of six to twelve people who perform similar or related work meet regularly to analyze and try to remedy "work-process problems"; the quality circles are credited with increasing productivity and generating significant savings (R. Denhardt, Pyle, & Bluedorn, 1987). Governance structures also frequently incorporate external interests. Ombudspersons, for instance, may provide early warning of clients' resistance or dissatisfaction, while shielding line workers from the demoralizing and time-consuming job of handling complaints. From an agency's perspective, "proxy advocates"—experts charged with representing citizen or consumer interests in complex areas like determining sites for nuclear power plants and setting utility rates (see, e.g., Gormley, 1986b)—may increase the quality of information available to decision makers and heighten support among constituents for the final decision.

Governance structures also offer means of interjecting "democracy," or employee participation, into the workplace. Private sector firms have introduced a variety of such practices, ranging from more consensual decision making and task sharing at lower levels to employee involvement in top management decisions (see, e.g., Kanter, 1983; J. O'Toole, 1985). Government agencies less frequently take these steps, in part because concern with "democracy" in the public sector typically emphasizes responsiveness to those *outside* of government. Even so, innovations like quality circles also promote greater employee participation in and control over their work environments.

The short-lived movement for a "New Public Administration" in the early 1970s tried to carry demands for "democratization" of government organizations further (see, e.g., Marini, 1971). Outraged by the continuing U.S. involvement in Vietnam despite massive public opposition, by what many perceived to be the stigmatizing treatment of welfare recipients, and by the rapidly dimming promise of a Great Society, some scholars blamed nonresponsive public agencies. Their proposed remedy was two-pronged. First, advocates of a New Public Administration argued for heightened participation by government workers in agency decision making. Bored and frustrated in stultifying hierarchies, bureaucrats allegedly felt little responsibility for their actions and little compulsion to lodge objections to policy decisions. Increasing their involvement in decision making at all levels, scholars contended, might enhance workers' sense of accountability for their actions. Second, the reformers pointed to the need for increased citizen participation in the formulation and delivery of programs that affected them, in order to heighten governmental responsiveness to clients' needs and demands. Only this latter proposal has had much lasting effect. Its legacy is seen today in the plethora of citizen advisory committees at all levels of government and in more limited attempts at "coproduction," in which bureaucrats, citizens, and other groups pool resources to rehabilitate houses in deteriorating central cities or build and operate park and recreation facilities (see, e.g., Ferris, 1984; Percy, 1983; Rich, 1981).

Although the specifics of the New Public Administration have faded, calls persist for additional governance structures to increase outside control of public organizations. As chapter 1 noted, a key recommendation following the *Challenger* disaster was for the creation of an external scientific advisory committee to evaluate NASA's technical decisions. Similarly, members of the House-Senate panel investigating the Iran-contra affair referred again and again to the need for vigorous congressional mechanisms to oversee intelligence operations; that the White House may have to establish similar structures might also be argued.

TOWARD A TYPOLOGY OF GOVERNANCE STRUCTURES

Although examples of governance structures abound in current work on organizations, references to them are scattered and mostly unconnected. Largely missing is a systematic presentation of an array of structures or an indication of the conditions under which they may be expected to emerge or might be most appropriate. We will postpone consideration of the latter questions until chapter 5 and explore, first, the range of possible governance structures.

Table 1 contains an initial inventory of such structures drawn from the literature on organizational decision making. The mechanisms are described in terms of several characteristics: the form of participation by organizational members and other actors, the type of expertise emphasized by the structure, the rules for making final decisions, and the ways in which each structure copes with conflict and uncertainty. Later chapters take up the assessment of these structures; here, we seek to provoke thinking about the numerous structural types that public agencies might use.

Before commenting briefly on each governance structure, we must reiterate that these are types of *structure*, not kinds of organization (cf. Hall,

TABLE 1 Characteristics of Selected Governance Structures

Characteristics	Governance Structure			
	Hierarchical	Adjudicative	Adversarial	Collegial-Competitive
Examples	Determination of food stamp eligibility; IRS audits	Administrative law hearings (e.g., appeals of denials of eligibility for Social Security disability payments); science courts	Structured bargaining; Executive Committee of the NSC	Regulatory negotiation; inclusion of "proxy advocates"
Characteristics				
Form of participation	Following or giving orders	Two-party advocacy	Multiparty advocacy	Advocacy of interests
Nature of expertise	Technical knowledge, organizational position	Skills in marshalling evidence, persuasion	Skills in marshalling evidence, persuasion	Political expertise (Cox & King, 1985), skills in persuasion and bargaining
Decision rule	Preference of top decision maker	Burden of proof (Fuller, 1978)	Judgment of decision maker (not included among advocates)	Majority/ extraordinary majority vote
Way of managing conflict	Resolution Avoidance (Thomas & Tymon, 1985)	Two-party competition	Multiparty competition	Competition Collaboration Compromise
Way of managing uncertainty	Resolution Avoidance	Reduction: Issues cast as right or wrong, correct or incorrect (Fuller, 1978; Popper, 1983)	Competition (may exacerbate uncertainty)	Competition Collaboration Compromise

(continued)

TABLE 1 *(continued)*

	Governance Structure		
	Collegial-Consensual	**Collegial-Mediative**	**Market**
Examples	*Ringi*; Wisconsin "consensus process"	Labor-management disputes; handling of New York City dispute over trash-to-energy plants; provisions in Age Discrimination Act	Coordination of San Francisco public transit system
Characteristics			
Form of participation	Cooperative search	Argument before neutral third party	Separate pursuit of different parties' objectives
Nature of expertise	Skills in persuasion, collaboration	Skills in mediation, argumentation	Little guaranteed, varies by party and situation
Decision rule	Consensus	Parties' acceptance or rejection of mediator's advice and proposed settlement	"Epiphenomenal coordination"
Way of managing conflict	Collaboration Avoidance ("groupthink"; Janis, 1972)	Guided compromise	Competition Avoidance
Way of managing uncertainty	Collaboration Avoidance	Guided compromise	Acceptance as inevitable

43

1987, p. 99). Any given organization may rely on a variety of governance structures, linked together in what chapter 7 will call *governance networks*. In addition, at this stage, we are discussing structures as *ideal types* (Weber, 1946), or analytical categories; we do not expect any of the mechanisms to operate exactly as described in any actual organization. Nor would we be surprised to find hybrids or structures with features that we have not entirely anticipated. Still, we believe the types presented do serve as useful stimulants to exploring the diversity of possible structures.

Hierarchical Structures

Probably the most common governance structure, hierarchy, vests ultimate authority and responsibility at the top, though some delegation of discretion to lower-level officials is common. Hierarchies are explicitly authoritarian: "information flows up, orders flow down." The alleged virtues of hierarchy have mainly to do with efficiency. With ends and means determined by top management, or else settled outside the organization (for example, by the mayor or Congress), hierarchy for many early management scientists was the preferred arrangement for attaining organizational goals at minimum cost. In public agencies, hierarchy has the added virtue of ensuring accountability to elected officials, thus promoting "overhead democracy" (Redford, 1969). As we have seen, for those who view organizations as control systems, hierarchy becomes almost synonymous with the formal organization.

The formal, or statutory, organization of government agencies is hierarchical, befitting the emphases on control and accountability that legislators insist upon. Nevertheless, within these hierarchical skeletons, a diversity of other structural arrangements for governance may be found.

Adjudicative Structures

Adjudicative structures are designed to handle recurring, legitimate disputes—legitimate in the sense that the parties in disagreement have an understood right to be heard. Detailed procedures provide an opportunity for participants to present their cases to a neutral decision maker, or "judge," who decides the case based on the facts and on arguments presented by the parties.[3] Observation of these often complex procedures is key to the legitimacy of adjudicative structures, and mastery of them is a powerful resource for participants. These mechanisms treat disputes as having only

3 Both adjudicative and hierarchical structures rely on a final decision maker to make authoritative choices. In a hierarchy, however, the inputs to that decision may come from a variety of sources. Further, what distinguishes hierarchy as a governance structure is the fact that being designated the decision maker authorizes one to make choices and give orders, bound only by the parameters of the authorization and the potential dissatisfaction of those higher up. In adjudicative structures, the decision maker is neutral and makes a decision on the basis of the case presented by the parties to the dispute. Another difference, of course, is that adjudicative structures presume conflict; hierarchical structures do not.

two sides, with outcomes generally cast as winning and losing, or right and wrong. The logic and operation of Anglo-American courts provide the model for adjudicative structures (cf. Schuck, 1979, p. 27).

Provisions for appealing denied Social Security disability claims are largely adjudicative in character. Claimants and caseworkers present evidence to a hearing examiner, who upholds or overturns the original decision (Mashaw, 1983). More novel are proposals for science courts, which would try to reach conclusions in disputes over scientific "facts" based on the contentions of opposing advocate scientists (see, e.g., Kantrowitz, 1977; Martin, 1979; Ozawa & Susskind, 1985; Yellin, 1983).

Adversarial Structures

An adversarial structure permits advocacy of more than two points of view. As in adjudicative structures, a neutral party ultimately renders a decision, as opposed to, for example, inducing compromise or consensus. Again, quality of argument and evidence is the primary resource for participants. Adversarial structures are preferred to adjudicative ones when disputes are difficult to cast in either-or terms (see, e.g., Fuller, 1978; Popper, 1983).

As attorney general, Elliot Richardson relied on an adversarial structure, the Executive Secretariat, "to force bureaucratic combatants to come together in the same room and argue out their differences openly"; Richardson then chose his desired policy option (Yates, 1985, p. 98). In a "purely adversarial" setting, "openly biased advocates urge their . . . cases before a passive decisionmaker" (Thibaut, Walker, & Lind, 1972, p. 388). More mixed is so-called structured bargaining, in which regulatory agencies gather disputants together to discuss their differences in an area of proposed government regulation. The agency not only sets the "policy parameters within which bargaining [is] conducted," but also is free to deviate from any understanding participants may reach (Schuck, 1979, p. 32; cf. Eisenberg, 1978).

Collegial-Competitive Structures

Collegial-competitive structures are modeled roughly upon legislative institutions. Like adversarial mechanisms, these structures permit the expression of multiple interests. Yet, unlike either adjudicative or adversarial structures, they do not provide for a neutral decision maker. Interests are advocated either directly or through representatives, with legitimacy being largely a function of the apparent openness and inclusiveness of the structure. Compromise or the development of consensus need not occur (though it may), necessitating formal rules, such as majority vote, for reaching closure. For a participant, "success" tends to reflect the capacity to persuade others that their interests are congruent with one's own rather than an ability to demonstrate the inherent merit of one's position.

In contrast to the more adjudicative procedures used in the United States, agencies in Western European countries tend to approach environmental regulation by allowing conflicting interest groups to discuss, and try to reach agreement on, various options *before* specific rules are promulgated (see, e.g., Piasecki & Gravander, 1985, p. 51). Even in the United States, "regulatory negotiation" is receiving increasing attention. In this kind of procedure, "interested parties seek to arrive at mutually acceptable policies through informal consultation and bargaining" (West, 1987, p. 23, note 25; cf. Fiorino, 1988; "Rethinking Regulation," 1981). For example, the Consumer Products Safety Commission, the Consumer Federation of America, and industry representatives formulated a new warning label and a program of consumer education for paint strippers, which contain methylene chloride, a suspected carcinogen (Stanfield, 1986, p. 2764). Similarly, the Environmental Protection Agency used regulatory negotiation to bring together representatives of industry, environmental groups, and state governments to produce a proposed rule to limit pollution from wood-burning stoves.

The EPA also uses collegial-competitive structures in strictly internal decision making. Its Steering Committee is composed of representatives of the six assistant administrators, the general counsel, and the relevant office directors. This body serves as a "forum for examining the development plan [for proposed regulations], resolving conflicts and problems, and assuring that legal requirements have been complied with" (Bryner, 1987, p. 102).

Collegial-Consensual Structures

In contrast, collegial-consensual structures work to fashion genuine agreement rather than to produce compromise decisions in the face of continuing disagreement. Such structures may range from periodic brainstorming sessions to more formal devices for eliciting and combining individual preferences and opinions (for example, the Delphi or Nominal Group techniques; see, e.g., Mahler, 1987).

Consensus building is familiar to those knowledgeable about Japanese management practices. *Ringi*, for instance, is a "collective decision-making process in which a policy document passes from manager to manager for approval . . . If a manager disagrees with what is being proposed, he [sic] is typically free to amend the decision proposal and to allow the document to circulate again" (G. Morgan, 1986, p. 93). Not only are consensual structures being adopted throughout the private sector in the United States, but the public sector is trying them as well. The Wisconsin legislature, for example, has experimented with a "consensus process" that joins legislators, lobbyists, and agency officials in an effort to formulate proposals that all can support. Gormley (1987, p. 163) reports that the mechanism has been used to pass laws regulating mining, water pollution, and unemployment compensation. Similarly, Friedman (1987) urges using advisory panels of experts to generate consensus on proposed regulations, based on the experience of the Nuclear Regulatory Commission in directing the cleanup of Three Mile Island.

Of the collegial structures, this one is most compatible with the basic assumptions of the view of organizations as control systems, since it may be used to eliminate acknowledged or perceived conflict and uncertainty. Top officials, for instance, might turn to collegial-consensual structures such as task forces and advisory boards as temporary, officially sanctioned respites from the routine workings of hierarchy.

Collegial-Mediative Structures

Like collegial-competitive mechanisms, mediative structures are designed to produce compromise. They pursue a form of consensus, but, unlike collegial-consensual structures, they generally aim at a consensus arrived at through tactical maneuvering rather than genuine opinion change, often one that is assumed to be temporary. Mediative structures are distinguished from competitive structures by their reliance on a neutral party—the mediator—who does not make the final decision but attempts to guide the disputants toward an acceptable compromise. The legitimacy of the process depends in large part on the participants' perceptions of the skill and fairness of the mediator. For instance, former Reagan National Security Adviser Frank Carlucci was credited with being an "honest broker" between Secretary of Defense Caspar Weinberger and Secretary of State George Schultz as they debated the pace and scope of development of the Strategic Defense Initiative (Kirschten, 1987a). Mediative structures also are used frequently in labor-management disputes and in local environmental controversies.

Examples of collegial-mediative mechanisms abound in the public sector. The Age Discrimination Act allows those alleging age discrimination and defendants to enter into mediation, with an independent body, the Federal Mediation and Conciliation Service, providing the mediator (Schuck, 1979, p. 33). Mediative structures also are frequently used in local environmental controversies (Schuck, 1979, p. 34). For instance, mediation helped settle a 1984 dispute over appropriate techniques for assessing the risks and health effects of trash-to-energy plants in New York City, as well as possible pollution-control strategies for the plants (Ozawa & Susskind, 1985). A variant of regulatory negotiation relies on an uninvolved agency official to serve as mediator; see, for example, Kettl's discussion of EPA's rule making for pesticides (1988, pp. 136–37).

Market Structures

In sharp contrast to all of these mechanisms are what we call *market structures* (cf. Stone, 1988). These structures permit decisions to emerge from the largely undirected interplay of individuals, groups, and subunits. Explicit questions of value or direction are never collectively raised, and coercion is minimal. The attainment of any collective interest or common objective is a by-product of participants' pursuit of their own interests. Although competition takes place in both market and collegial-competitive structures, market structures have no rules regulating decision closure and tend not to specify who must participate.

Market mechanisms in organizations may not really seem to be structures at all, at least in the conventional sense in which most of us use the term. But a "market" strategy for handling policy problems may recur in organizations, making it a form of political structuring. The almost random flows of "people, problems, and solutions" tracked by the "organized anarchy" model of organizations (e.g., Cohen, March, & Olsen, 1976) resemble the undirected dynamics of a market. Often, too, organizations intentionally avoid coordination and confrontation as a means of absorbing or "quasi-resolving" conflict (cf. Cyert & March, 1963; March & Simon, 1958). Bendor's (1985) portrait of the highly complex system of public and private mass transportation in the San Francisco Bay Area may be understood in these terms, with little overt coordination among the major actors and considerable redundancy of operation. Coordination occurs but it is largely unintentional, or epiphenomenal.

We have seen that structure is a key concern for those who study, work in, and seek to redirect organizations. The notion of governance structures trains our attention on the patterned channeling of politics in organizations. Although works in organization theory and public administration are studded with references to diverse structures, few systematic examinations of structural types can be found. This chapter began the task of exploring different governance mechanisms. Yet, no matter how complete such a typology may be, classification alone is not very satisfying. A concern with developing organization policy points to more pressing questions. What are the consequences of varying structures? Which mechanisms are appropriate under what circumstances? Why do certain kinds of structures seem to emerge under particular conditions? We turn next to these issues.

CHAPTER FOUR

Organizational Decision Settings: Confronting Uncertainty and Controversy

We have asserted that structure matters, at least when one focuses upon governance structures and politically relevant outcomes. Chapter 3 pointed to a variety of possible governance structures. To get a better sense of how these diverse structures might arise, and when they might be most appropriate, we need to probe more deeply into the decision settings that public organizations confront. As chapter 2 hinted, such exploration brings us face to face with considerable turbulence both inside and outside government agencies. Mandates are often vague and inconsistent, policy problems only dimly understood or formulated in contradictory ways. Meanwhile, elected officials, clients, constituents, and the public at large may be clamoring for action, sharply split over necessary responses or vacillating in offering direction or support.

This chapter examines the sources of uncertainty and controversy over policy goals and techniques. Chapter 5 pursues the implications of controversy and uncertainty for governmental structuring and response.

ORGANIZATIONAL DECISION SETTINGS

Before we can fully examine the link between decision setting and organizational structure, we must consider the problems organizations face. Yet the policy predicaments in which government agencies become enmeshed are difficult to capture in any simple classification. Policy arenas differ dramatically in the number and kind of participants, ranging from tightly coupled "iron triangles," with their small and closed memberships, to more open "elastic nets," crowded with a continually changing cast of characters (e.g., Heclo, 1978; Jordan, 1981). Policy problems also vary—for example, in their salience to key actors, public visibility, complexity, and distributional characteristics (see, e.g., Gormley & Peters, 1987; Ripley & Franklin, 1984).

Here, we will follow the lead of many organization theorists and focus on the degree of uncertainty and controversy organizations face as they strive to set goals and determine how to attain them. Although this approach excludes some of the empirical richness of actual decision settings, it allows us to grab hold analytically of key features of policy processes and to trace out their implications.

Goals and Technologies

Like eminent organization theorists Herbert Simon (1947) and James Thompson and Arthur Tuden (1959), we distinguish between preferences about possible outcomes, or *goals*, and beliefs about cause-effect relationships, or *technologies*. In this view, decision making involves both articulating goals and selecting among means for attaining them.

Around the country, for instance, city governments wrestle with the problems of the homeless (see, e.g., Moore, Sink, & Hoban-Moore, 1988). At first glance, the goals of such efforts seem clear: to get people off the streets, improving their living conditions without overburdening the taxpayers. Translating these goals into concrete programs, however, reveals a jumble of possible objectives and values for assessing government action. Residents and owners of small businesses may emphasize quick and forceful removal of transients. Others place higher priority on finding the homeless emergency food and medical care; longer-term shelter needs assume secondary importance. Still others worry about how to help the homeless move toward self-sufficiency, which may mean not only finding them temporary housing but also training, jobs, treatment for alcohol or drug abuse, or psychiatric care. All the while, government officials try to keep their programs from attracting the needy from other communities, and civil libertarians strive to protect the rights of the homeless to choose how they will live.

Cities have experimented with numerous ways of addressing at least some of these demands—conducting police sweeps of skid rows and neighborhood parks, supporting soup kitchens and mobile medical services, establishing temporary encampments, opening public buildings for sleeping, building more permanent shelters, offering transition housing. Clearly, some of the underlying goals of these efforts are rather vague (does "self-sufficiency" mean holding a job or qualifying for welfare?). Other goals may conflict—for example, removing the homeless from the streets versus protecting their civil rights. Similarly, the suggested remedies, or policy "technologies," provide few guarantees that they will solve or even reduce the problems, and such proposals have sparked controversy in cities from Los Angeles to New York. In short, governments are sure neither what to do about the homeless nor how to do it. Both goals and technologies confront public organizations with significant problems.

Controversy and Uncertainty

The importance of policy goals and technologies to understanding governmental decision making seems clear. The next step is to find terms with which to analyze them. Typically, scholars have distinguished between goal consensus and controversy, and between technical certainty and uncertainty (e.g., Douglas & Wildavsky, 1982; Stout, 1980; J. Thompson, 1967; J. Thompson & Tuden, 1959). The governance model goes one step further, arguing that both ends and means may be characterized by their degree of certainty (or consensus), uncertainty, and controversy. *Controversy* implies that two or more actors are to some extent "certain" of their own positions, but have differing views. In contrast, *uncertainty* refers to circumstances in which participants are genuinely in doubt. *Goal* uncertainty may reflect the absence of a clear legislative mandate or of operational definitions of policy objectives, such as "maximum feasible participation" by citizens in community development programs; it also may result from organizational confusion in the face of multiple, incompatible goals. Under conditions of *technical* uncertainty, parties to a decision "[do] not know the probabilities connecting behavioral choices and environmental outcomes" (March & Simon, 1958, p. 113; cf. Arrow, 1974, pp. 33–34).

Clearly, technical matters often are ambiguous, but in other cases they are very much in dispute. Such disagreement helps account for a great deal of the debate over President Reagan's Strategic Defense Initiative ("Star Wars"), for example, and for the pitched battles between proponents of cash assistance for those needing income support and advocates of so-called workfare. The difficulty in such cases is not that everyone agrees that "we don't know how" to address particular policy problems; rather, many think that they *do* know, but the proposed approaches conflict.

Conversely, disputes over goals are familiar. But it is also true that goals may be unclear without being actively controversial. Public welfare policy in the United States, for instance, tends to be freighted with objectives ranging from providing a subsistence standard of living, to encouraging the "work ethic" by requiring able-bodied recipients to perform some work in return for assistance, to ensuring that public monies are used as intended (through, for example, provision of food stamps and housing vouchers, with follow-ups by caseworkers). All these goals are laudable; which of them do or should direct government programs is much less clear. Despite the goal uncertainty and technical controversy, however, most citizens expect government to pursue some sort of social welfare policy.

Sources of Controversy and Uncertainty

The emphasis in this discussion is on the level and nature of the uncertainty and controversy that prevail *within* organizations. The *sources* of ambiguity and conflict, however, may be either internal or external. For instance, internal uncertainty may reflect outside controversy over acceptable policy goals or feasible technologies. External conflict also may breed controversy inside an agency as advocates emerge to pursue policy options pressed by constituents in the environment. At the same time, uncertainties and conflicts may arise in organizations without being triggered by outside catalysts. Disputes within one state planning office over whether it should be a "line" agency with operating responsibilities or a "staff" unit advising the governor seemed arcane and largely irrelevant to outside observers but generated considerable internal controversy (Hult, 1987).

Elaborating upon the possible sources of goal and technical uncertainty and controversy should help to clarify these concepts and highlight the challenges they pose for public policy making and for government organizations. First, however, we should caution that the distinction between uncertainty and controversy is *analytical*, not empirical. Conceptually, it seems to us to make sense to distinguish between situations in which goals or technologies are unclear and those in which people disagree over appropriate objectives or technologies. As we shall suggest in chapter 5, uncertainty and controversy may call for different approaches to decision making. When there is uncertainty, efforts to gather more information, to probe for alternatives, and to explore consequences seem to be called for. Under conditions of controversy, it is likely to be more important to assure that different points of view are aired and attempts made to evaluate and choose among them, perhaps by compromise, perhaps through authoritative decision. Empirically, of course, uncertainty and controversy may be difficult to untangle. Uncertainty may trigger controversy as participants explore varying ways of coping with it. From an agency's perspective, external controversy may enmesh it in uncertainty, providing no clear direction for its actions. Moreover, as chapter 6 will elaborate, *perceptions* of uncertainty and controversy are important; participants may define as conflict what appears to an observer to be uncertainty. Nevertheless, for theoretical purposes, explicitly distinguishing between the two seems warranted: it may sharpen our understanding of the problem settings that organizations confront and lead to the design of better ways of coping with the uncertainties and controversies that so often face government.

SETTING ORGANIZATIONAL GOALS

That the goals of government agencies are frequently ambiguous or conflicting is a staple of policy research and public criticism. The U.S. Department of Housing and Urban Development, for example, is charged with providing "a decent home and a suitable living environment" for all Americans, a mission subject to myriad and not always consistent interpretations. Meanwhile, the Department of Health and Human Services struggles to fund and oversee family planning programs amidst demands that it foster "family participation" in teenage contraception decisions, promote chastity, cut adolescent pregnancy rates, discourage abortion, and address the burgeoning problem of sexually transmitted diseases such as AIDS. As the discussion below suggests, uncertainty about and controversy over policy goals flow from a variety of sources.

Goal Uncertainty

Uncertainty about goals has roots inside and outside of organizations. It results in part from the unclear and fluctuating demands placed upon public agencies by those outside, a situation James Thompson has termed "contingency" (1967, p. 159). Since elections can produce changes in political leadership and policy direction, public organizations face the prospect of inherent uncertainty. With the election of Ronald Reagan in 1980, for example, the Environmental Protection Agency was presented with new goals, expected to pursue economic as well as environmental objectives. Increasingly unclear was how the agency would juggle the multiple goals pressed upon it—protecting the physical environment, preserving jobs in polluting industries, refraining from interfering with economic growth and development.

Moreover, the statutes directing agency activities are often vague. The Clean Air Act, for instance, instructed the EPA to enforce industry use of the "best available control technology" but provided little guidance for defining either "best" or "available" (Greenwood, 1984, p. 47).

Nor are the courts always clearer. Since federal district and appellate courts can and often do decide cases on different grounds, agencies may have little clear guidance on which to base their actions. "Those looking for babble can do no better than to consult the inferior federal judiciary, whose opinions contradict each other on important questions aplenty" (Easterbrook, 1987, p. 56). Agencies also continually face the possibility that long months of work may be overturned in the courts, a potent source of uncertainty.

An agency's constituencies may level equally ambiguous demands. Especially as problems grow in complexity, pressures may mount for agencies to "do something," with little specification of what that something might be or what criteria should be used to evaluate different courses of action. Although policy issues such as education, welfare, and deficit reduction all provoke passionate debate, they also generate considerable uncertainty for government agencies, for clear directions or priorities rarely emerge from such discussions.

Further complications arise from *internal* sources of ambiguity. High turnover rates among political appointees may leave units rudderless. Additional uncertainty may flow from the tendency of all complex organizations to divide labor and hence foster specialization. Organizational subunits with differing objectives and priorities may leave top decision makers in a quandary about which direction to take; meanwhile, subunits may confront uncertainty about the likely reactions of other units to their aims and priorities.

Goal Controversy

At other times, goals are controversial. When conflict is present, varying interpretations of goals find advocates within an organization, and bureaucrats seek to impose their own preferences. In contrast, under conditions of uncertainty officials search for ways of responding to ambiguous goals or try to reconcile multiple objectives.

Controversy over goals arises from sources similar to those fostering goal uncertainty. Among *external* sources, outsiders may press inconsistent, conflicting demands on government organizations. Legislators, for example, often appear to insist upon contradictory objectives. Thus, officials of the Social Security Administration's disability program face almost irreducible goal conflict: in effect, Congress has instructed the SSA to " 'help the poor but punish the chiselers' " in making eligibility decisions and setting benefit levels (Mashaw, 1983, p. 19).

The courts foster additional goal conflict. In his study of the enforcement of the Clean Air Act, R. Shep Melnick found that firms protesting the costs of complying with EPA regulations and environmentalists challenging rules of general applicability sought redress in different courts. This state of affairs "allowed courts hearing enforcement cases [brought by firms] to ignore their effect on air quality and courts hearing cases on general policy [filed by environmentalists] to ignore questions of cost and feasibility" (1983, p. 345). The EPA, meanwhile, was left with conflicting directives, a situation that in turn generated controversy within the agency, with each side armed with court decisions as ammunition.

In addition, an agency's constituents may push it to pursue inconsistent objectives. By the 1980s, NASA was juggling demands from within the federal government that it both maintain its safety record and carry out military (or "dark") missions. At the same time it was seeking to respond to commercial customers complaining about mounting costs and unreliable shuttle scheduling as well as to scientists pushing the agency to honor its commitments to further basic research (for example, by placing the long-delayed space telescope in orbit).

Another external source of controversy may be the disjunction between environmental directives and the professional norms of agency officials. A policy analyst steeped in the use of rigorous and complicated quantitative techniques may discover that concern with their "proper" application is at odds with the insistence of elected officials or political appointees on "quick and dirty" analyses that yield speedier and more easily communicated results. Responsiveness to the legitimate demands of elected officials and their constituents often may conflict with analysts' commitment to professional standards. The result may be acrimonious disagreements between "generalists" and "specialists."

Internal sources of conflict also may be present. Turnover among political appointees can trigger intense battles over turf and policy direction. In addition, specialization may induce overcommitment to the subgoals pursued by the various specialists, as well as conflict between these goals (e.g., Cyert & March, 1963; March & Simon, 1958). Local bureaucrats responsible for making loans to small businesses may well come to equate "community development" with "neighborhood economic development," while officials allocating grants for housing rehabilitation stress residential revitalization (e.g., Hult, 1987). Neither group is incorrect, but a community development agency's efforts to set priorities may plunge into virtual street fighting over the organization's mission.

Differing professional orientations in an organization may provoke similar controversy over the organization's direction. In 1982, the Office of Adolescent Pregnancy Programs (OAPP, located in the U.S. Department of Health and Human Services) proposed a regulation requiring that parents be notified when their minor children received prescription contraceptives from federally funded family planning clinics. In analyzing the rule, departmental lawyers focused immediately on its likely effects on judicially established rights and duties, such as a teenager's privacy and parents' responsibilities for their children's health. Public health professionals, in contrast, emphasized the possibility that the rule might inhibit teenage contraceptive use, boost the adolescent pregnancy rate, and lead to physical abuse of children by angry parents. Both the lawyers and the public health experts had their own characteristic, professionally prescribed notions of OAPP's primary goals, notions that reinforced internal questions about the wisdom of the proposed rule (see Hult, 1988).

Controversy also may result from inconsistencies between an agency's orientations and external demands and expectations. An EPA populated by those firmly committed to the environmentalist goals of the 1960s and 1970s found it difficult to adapt to the views of Reagan administration officials (Kraft & Vig, 1983). This tension triggered sharp exchanges betweeen political appointees and civil servants, and likely provoked disputes among the permanent bureaucrats over the appropriate balance between responsiveness to political appointees (and hence to the president) and responsibilities to ongoing programs (and thus to some extent to Congress; Wood, 1988).

SELECTING POLICY TECHNOLOGIES

Even when goals are clear and few disagree, the means of attaining them may be obscure or controversial. Technical uncertainty and controversy abound in the public sector; indeed, the most difficult technical problems are often those left to government.

In many policy arenas, the state of the art is incomplete and rudimentary, and the effects of particular policy interventions are difficult to predict and often disputed, especially as one looks further into the future or beyond "first order" consequences. This situation takes one into the realm of what Alvin Weinberg has called "trans-science," where "questions of fact . . . are unanswerable by science" (1979, p. 209). Nor does understanding cause–effect links always guarantee that policies will produce the intended outcomes, for government agencies rarely control all the factors that influence the results of interventions (see, e.g., Mazmanian & Sabatier, 1981).

Education provides a good illustration of some of these difficulties. Educators know relatively little about how to curb the mounting high school dropout rates in many major cities. Even as understanding grows, though, local school officials might be hard pressed to make much headway. They can do little to anticipate or compensate for such variables as fluctuating state or federal funding, the influence of particular teachers and counselors, the differential effects of family and peers on potential dropouts, or shifts in the availability of jobs for high school graduates.

As with goal uncertainty and controversy, uncertainty about and controversy over policy technologies arise from a number of sources.

Technical Uncertainty

Technical uncertainty flows from many sources *outside* the organization. First, as Ted Greenwood (1984) suggests, deficient scientific knowledge can produce considerable ambiguity. Sometimes little information about a problem exists. At present, for example, there are 4.5 million known chemicals, 45,000 of which are in common use; yet reliable tests have been done on only a small fraction of them. No one knows for sure how many dangerous chemicals there are or how to prioritize those that might pose risks. Thus, untested carcinogens "overwhelm whatever is known about safety" (Douglas & Wildavsky, 1982, p. 53).

In other cases, information is available but ambiguous. Epidemiological studies of the effects of known carcinogens on humans—that is, analyses relying on human mortality and morbidity rates—are notoriously difficult to interpret (Greenwood, 1984, p. 72). Based on small samples and often questionable certifications of the cause of death, these analyses are of dubious reliability, as the researchers who do them are quick to admit. Moreover, the studies leave open the possibility that death or disease resulted from exposure to several chemicals rather than the one being focused upon, or that the group studied was not typical of the population of interest to regulators.

Perhaps even more troubling, some information is inherently unobtainable. To be reliable, estimates of the risks of a nuclear power plant disaster, for instance, would need to be based on experience with the same size and type of plant over a period of hundreds or thousands of years (see, e.g., Perrow, 1984, p. 33).

Second, even when usable data are available, suitable techniques for analyzing them may not be. Those seeking to assess the risks of hazardous chemicals struggle continually with how to estimate the impact of lower levels of exposure using data on the health effects of much higher doses. How to move from tests with laboratory animals to predictions for human beings is likewise unclear (e.g., Hoel & Crump, 1981; Ozawa & Susskind, 1985). These are not merely academic issues: different techniques may produce dramatically different results. Comparisons of risk extrapolations calculated by the National Academy of Science and the EPA's Carcinogen Assessment Group revealed differences as large as a factor of 100 in *both* directions (suggesting little systematic bias; Kimm, Kuzmack, & Schnare, 1981, p. 238). Estimates of the risk of cancer from PCBs (polychlorinated biphenyls) have ranged from 7.2 cancers per 100,000 people by the Food and Drug Administration to 450 cancers per 100,000 according to EPA (J. Lawler & Parle, 1988, p. 8).

Rapid technological advances produce other uncertainties. Charles Perrow worries that experiments with recombinant DNA may be outstripping human capacity to understand the dynamics of creating new life forms. Thus, the release of large quantities of new organisms (for example, to protect strawberries from frost or clean up an oil spill) "may produce totally unexpected interactions. There is simply nothing in our experience to go by" (1984, p. 298; but see Lustick, 1980, p. 348).

Experience, of course, may only muddy our understanding of policy dynamics. As frequently as local, state, and national agencies have turned to employment training programs, it is unclear whether such programs contribute much to placing people in stable jobs or, if they do, which approaches work best. Paul Sabatier argues more generally that learning from experience

> is very difficult in a world where performance gaps are difficult to measure, well-developed causal theories are often lacking, controlled experimentation is virtually impossible, opponents are doing everything possible to muddle the situation and otherwise impede one from learning, and even allies' motives are often suspect because of personal and organizational rivalries. (1987, p. 675)

Moreover, given the interdependence of many physical and social processes, attempts to address one problem may produce others. A classic example is public assistance. Intended to provide relatively short-term aid for those facing difficulties such as unemployment, illness, or the death or departure of a breadwinner, welfare may reduce incentives for some recipients (though by no means all) to seek work. Over time, receiving welfare may affect the willingness to work not only of household heads but also of their dependents, transforming episodic assistance to ongoing support. That the validity of such an interpretation has been questioned only spotlights the swirling uncertainty long characteristic of this policy arena.

Nor do unanticipated and undesired consequences plague only social policy. Chlorination of water was similarly well-intended, meant to protect the public from disease-carrying organisms. Yet chlorine may interact with organic compounds to produce chloroform and other trihalomethanes, all suspected carcinogens (Crandall & Lave, 1981; Page, Harris, & Bruser, 1981, p. 220).

Thus, external technical uncertainty often pervades agency decision making. Uncertainties also may arise *internally*. Limited time and funds, for example, may restrict the search for information and clarifying analyses, magnifying perceived uncertainty. Experts within agencies may compound the uncertainty facing top decision makers by adding to or elaborating upon ambiguous interpretations.

Technical Controversy

Perhaps not surprisingly, inadequate information, unproven techniques, ambiguous findings, and complex policy dynamics do not always keep participants in policy debates from promoting their preferred options with confidence and certainty. Experts frequently disagree over appropriate methods for risk assessment, each advocating preferred approaches (see, e.g., Hattis & Kennedy, 1986). Different professional groups may well believe that their approach to a problem is more valid. Meanwhile, the absence of appropriate internal expertise may deprive agency officials of the ability to separate policy-relevant disputes from intramural quarreling among outside experts.

In addition, efforts by interest groups to mobilize their members and attract public support may lead them to exaggerate the certainty of their claims about the benefits and costs of particular policy technologies. The Tobacco Institute's long-standing insistence that smoking is not linked to cancer falls into this category (see Fritschler, 1983). Similarly, elected officials may discover that staking out a definite position in a dispute focuses public attention and support more readily than does a discussion of uncertainties and complexities.

Controversy also may arise when "experts" and the public apply different standards in determining "acceptable" uncertainties (see, e.g., Douglas & Wildavsky, 1982; Perrow, 1984). Those living near the site of a proposed nuclear power plant, for example, may be less tolerant of inherently uncertain predictions about the possibility of serious accidents than are those who generate the estimates.

Finally, of course, experts within agencies may fan the flames of outside debates, serving as advocates for conflicting positions. This source of controversy may be heightened when subunits have competing interests. During the Carter administration, for example, the new chairman of the Federal Trade Commission confronted an agency with a general counsel wary of hostile courts, an Office of Policy Planning that was "free market-minded [and] skeptical," and a dedicated bloc of consumerists (Heymann, 1987, pp. 34ff). The result was considerable internal conflict over such proposals as restricting advertising on children's programs.

Any of these factors may spark explosive technical controversy, often with significant implications for decision making. One apparently arcane scientific dispute revolves around the "epigenetic" and "genotoxic" theories of cell chemistry. The former argues that some carcinogens affect cell mechanisms other than DNA strands, which are responsible for cell reproduction; the latter maintains that all carcinogens alter genetic materials in cells. From the vantage point of a regulatory body like the EPA, this controversy points to a crucial choice: the epigenetic theory indicates that humans might be exposed to greater amounts of some carcinogens without fear of cancer, while the genotoxic view suggests the need for stricter regulation (Waterman, 1987, p. 4). EPA Administrator Anne Gorsuch Burford became embroiled in intense debate when she steered the agency toward the first, less restrictive position (cf. Burford, 1986).

As this chapter's brief excursion suggests, goal and technical uncertainty and controversy may arise from many sources inside and outside of organizations. Agencies frequently find themselves pursuing policies with multiple, ill-defined, and sometimes conflicting goals; relying upon ambiguous or controversial policy technologies; and confronting numerous clients, constituents, and overseers as well as their own panoply of experts. With Henry Aaron, one can ask rather plaintively: "What is an ordinary member of the tribe to do when the witch doctors disagree?" (1978, p. 159). Even more sobering, what happens when even the witch doctors are unsure and not everyone is certain they are the right ones to ask?

Unless one believes that government should take action only when consensus reigns, when values can be prioritized, and when options come stamped with guarantees, decision making under conditions of goal and technical uncertainty and controversy cannot be avoided. Indeed, the need for thinking about how organizations should respond in such circumstances may be growing (cf. Kraus, 1980). Certainly, much governmental activity has relatively clear and agreed-upon goals and routine, well-understood technologies—for example, issuing Social Security checks on time or allocating sewer grants according to legislatively prescribed formulas. Yet, as we have seen, uncertainty and conflict flow from many sources, and at least in the short to medium run they may be irreducible (cf. Dror, 1986; Landau & Stout, 1979). Moreover, government's most important tasks—for instance, implementing the amnesty program for illegal aliens, protecting the environment, educating children—will likely also be those that generate the most controversy and confusion (cf. Gawthrop, 1984, pp. 91–92). In the next chapter, we explore how differing governance structures might help public organizations respond to these challenges.

Responding to Uncertainty and Controversy: The Search for Appropriate Governance Structures

We have now gathered the pieces of our puzzle: an initial inventory of the types of governance structures that organizations might employ and a sense of the diverse decision settings confronted by public agencies. The next step is to put the pieces together.

Our discussion thus far helps account for the emergence of governance structures. Still open, however, are the questions of *which* structures arise under particular circumstances and of which structures *ought* to arise. This chapter takes up the latter issue. After exploring the notion of "appropriate" structuring, we present an argument for the governance structures that seem best suited for various decision settings. Our examination highlights the potential importance of these structures in helping organizations cope with uncertainty and controversy, and it suggests the broader effects of structure on organizational political systems.

THE QUESTION OF APPROPRIATENESS

We begin with the premise that decision setting and governance structure should be *congruent* (cf. Nadler & Tushman, 1980). We assume, that is, that in particular settings certain structures will be more or less appropriate in shaping the organization's response. In this section, we examine the possible meanings of structural "appropriateness." As we shall soon see, this is a notoriously slippery notion whose meaning may well differ from one context to another.

We first should make clear that, although we believe there should be some match between decision problem and organizational structure, our position is not one of environmental determinism—the stance, for example, of some natural system theorists (e.g., Hannan & Freeman, 1978a; Katz & Kahn, 1978; cf. Abrahamson, 1977, pp. 122–23, and Van de Ven, 1983, p. 44). We do not claim that congruent structures will always arise or that a process of natural selection will cause certain structures, and only those structures, to endure. Instead, we offer a *prescriptive* argument: other things being equal, organizations can better address policy problems if their structures are better able to cope with a variety of decision settings. As an empirical matter, however, we will contend in chapter 6 that the structural diversity one now observes in organizations does not fully reflect the range of settings organizations confront. Structures that fail to meet our criteria of appropriateness will be found in many contexts. One reason for this lack of congruence, as the careful reader will have noted, is that "other things" are never equal. Factors other than governance structures and the goal and technical uncertainty and controversy reviewed in the last chapter also mold decisions. "Street-level bureaucrats," for example, may transform or simply ignore orders from headquarters; on some highly salient issues, the public may demand quick and vigorous action by high-level officials, no matter how technically complex the underlying problem or how obscure the likely consequences of possible responses. Furthermore, structures inevitably *shape* as well as *respond to* perceived policy problems.

Still, we believe that appropriate governance structures can be prescribed for particular decision settings. Before examining these proposed links more fully, we need to elaborate the notion of appropriateness.

Appropriate Decision Structures: A Process View

Our understanding of appropriateness flows from the assumption that policy making should be judged primarily on the basis of the decision *process* rather than on the nature of the *outcome*. (As we shall see, however, not all agree with such a view of appropriateness.) Especially as uncertainty or controversy grows, it becomes increasingly difficult to determine in advance what will constitute "good" policy in substantive terms. When, for example, cause-and-effect links are ambiguous and thus reasonable aspirations for policy are uncertain, or when goals are multiple and competing, those trying to assess organizational decision making may be more justified in relying on "process values" (see, e.g., Chamberlin & Jackson, 1987, pp. 593–94; Mashaw, 1985). Robert Bell makes explicit the underlying expectation: "if [policy] deliberation is sound, organizations should arrive at appropriate decisions" (1985, p. 24; cf. Wamsley, 1984, p. 26).

Notice that this reasoning is consistent with our understanding of organizations as political systems. In national polities like the United States, we routinely admit that goals (or "the public interest") are diffuse and usually negotiable. This situation places a premium on the processes by which goals are established, challenged, and reestablished. Legitimacy derives largely from the manner in which goals are determined, rather than from the content of the resulting commitments. Thus, democratic theorists often associate legitimacy with acceptable procedures—and by implication with appropriate structures and institutions—rather than with any particular goal or policy outcome. "[I]n the end [people] rely on faith that administrators will be good stewards when exercising judgment about right and wrong, or good and bad decisions" (Mitchell & Scott, 1987, p. 448; cf. Heymann, 1987, p. 42).

Process is also important when the *means* for achieving goals are unclear or disputed. Judith Gruber argues, for example:

> The goal of liberty may . . . be paramount in policy areas with highly uncertain technologies . . . Where we lack confidence in our ability to achieve a collective end, would-be controllers may consider safeguards against harmful government action to be particularly important. (1987, p. 136)

Process Values

Assuming the importance of assessing process, what are the desirable features of policy decision making and hence of the structures that shape it? We will emphasize four evaluative criteria, all familiar to students of politics and policy making: bureaucratic rationality, accountability, representativeness, and legitimacy. In doing so, we try to avoid the trap Kathy Ferguson warns against: "[Organization theorists] stumble into the most elementary insights of political theory with great fanfare, reinventing conceptual wheels" (1984, p. 80). Instead, we seek to use those insights to provide a foundation for our exploration of organizational governance.

Bureaucratic rationality. "Bureaucratic rationality" will seem an awkward term to some, an oxymoron to others. We use it in a way similar to that of Jerry Mashaw (1983) in his analysis of the Social Security Administration's disability program. Mashaw stresses the importance of incorporating relevant expertise and information into agency decision making. Doing so arguably enhances what Oliver Williamson calls "procedural rationality," which involves ensuring that "the relevant dimensions [of policy issues] are identified and ordered and that indirect consequences are described in a way that can contribute to a well-considered public policy" (1981b, p. 132). Although there are few guarantees, observers of both the public and private sectors are beginning to suggest that structures that increase an organization's ability to search for and consider a wide range of information may lead to improved performance (e.g., Gawthrop, 1984; J. O'Toole, 1985). What seems to be needed more generally are structures that help decision makers define and interpret problems in ways that are appropriate to or congruent with the decision setting.

This should not be taken as a counsel of perfection, however. Clearly, scarce time and energy, insufficient expertise, and lack of available knowledge militate against the consideration of "all" information. Moreover, human cognitive limitations and rapidly changing policy environments place what are likely to be inherent limits on decision making. Thus, a second component of bureaucratic rationality is the ability to reach closure, to come to a decision (or to decide *not* to decide) even in the absence of certainty that all data and policy options have been examined, or of consensus on their interpretations or on the action to be taken.

Bureaucratic rationality, then, makes severe demands on governance structures. Structures must both encourage wide-ranging search when decisions seem to require it and guide decision making when the search yields few definitive answers or triggers controversy. Desirable structures are "rational," for they promote consideration of available facts, policy alternatives, and possible consequences. Yet they cannot be "objectively rational" (Simon, 1976), given the many constraints on organizational decision making.

Accountability. Complications deepen when one turns to the second process value. Accountability to the citizenry is a major concern in political systems that consider themselves democracies. We use the term *accountability* to refer to the capacity of elected officials (acting on behalf of the voters) or their delegates (such as personal staffers and political appointees) to monitor and, when necessary, redirect the activities of an agency or one of its subunits. From the perspective of the agency, accountability gets at its degree of "answerability" to elected officials and, through them, to the general public.

Seen in this way, "democratic" accountability often seems to require hierarchical structures and top-down control. Yet these do not appear to be necessary conditions for accountability. Most generally, accountability means that persons or units can be held responsible—that is, held "to account"—for their actions; it involves the "identifiability of particular individuals or groups who are the effective causes" of organizational actions (Pennock, 1979, p. 267). Many different governance structures conceivably could meet such requirements.

Structures with relatively high accountability may promote bureaucratic rationality. Paying attention to the demands of elected officials, for example, may provide decision makers with a better sense of the extent of financial and political support they can count on for various policy options. Continual reexamination by external overseers also may enhance an organization's ability to recognize and correct errors (cf. Landau, 1973). At the same time, elected officials may insist on results that experts find unreasonable or undesirable, or they may contribute to delays. In such cases, accountability is heightened at the expense of bureaucratic rationality (cf. Yates, 1982, pp. 153–54).

Representativeness. The third process value, representativeness, leads to further complexity. This standard directs attention, first, to the inclusiveness of the decision process, pointing to the importance of participation by those who may be affected by the decision and by those whose assent appears to be critical to the acceptability of both the policy process and the decision outcome (see, e.g., Fritschler, 1983, pp. 145–46; Ozawa & Susskind, 1985, p. 26; Redford, 1969, p. 44; Williamson, 1981b, p. 143; Yellin, 1983, pp. 1326–27). Which parties should be included in a decision structure will vary according to whether the decision problem involves goals or technologies. For example, conflict over or uncertainty about *goals* indicates the need for representation of concerned "stakeholders," those with interests in relevant policy goals and organizational missions. When controversy or ambiguity revolves around *technology*, representation of experts seems critical, and representativeness becomes identical with bureaucratic rationality. Participation by generalists such as elected officials, political appointees, and citizens also should be maintained, given concerns with preserving accountability. Including generalists may have the added advantage of keeping the agency from being "captured" by the interests it serves; such capture can undercut bureaucratic rationality and overly restrict representation. Indeed, John Burke (1986, p. 212) argues that agency officials bear a special responsibility for expanding the scope of representation. They should work, for example, to include those who otherwise might not participate, such as consumers or residents of poor neighborhoods.

Representativeness, however, involves more than merely providing access to the policy arena. It also requires what Hanna Pitkin calls "potential responsiveness." Although participants need not always gain their preferred outcomes, their input should be actively considered, not "frustrate[d] or resist[ed] systematically over a long period of time" (Pitkin, 1967, p. 233).

Clearly, concerns with representativeness and bureaucratic rationality may be mutually reinforcing. Broadening participation in decision making may increase the range of information and policy options available to decision makers, pointing to possible innovations or unforeseen difficulties, or alerting them to potential problems in gaining compliance. One of the reasons for promoting "citizen participation" in much of the community-development decision making of the 1960s and 1970s, for example, was to incorporate the residents' understanding of the specific problems their neighborhoods faced. Federal officials realized, too, that without such involvement many revitalization efforts would wither from lack of support, if not active hostility.

At the same time, the search for representative structures may hamper the pursuit of bureaucratic rationality and accountability. Citizen organizations have been accused of delaying many projects, thus defeating efforts to achieve decision closure. They also may reduce accountability; the Community Action Program virtually barred local elected officials from participating in decisions affecting their cities. If representation is restricted to those who can organize effectively to articulate their particularistic interests, decisions may be contrary to the overall interests of citizens, as critics of "interest group liberalism" (Lowi, 1979) and the "social pork barrel" (Stockman, 1975) contend. Nor do "interested" groups always present policy makers with useful information. Some of those commenting on the parental notification rule discussed in chapter 4 misread the proposed regulation, believing that it required parental consent before teenagers received contraceptives or that it restricted adolescents' access to abortion. Others insisted that the availability of contraceptives increased teenage pregnancy rates, in the absence of any supporting evidence. Meanwhile, the Office of Adolescent Pregnancy Programs resolutely ignored statutory law and legislative history that expressly prohibited the proposed rule (cf. *Planned Parenthood v. Schweiker*, 559 F.Supp. 658, 1983; 712 F.2d. 650, 1983; *State of New York v. Schweiker*, 557 F.Supp. 354, 1983).

Legitimacy. The point is not that representativeness should be sacrificed to bureaucratic rationality or accountability, or that any one of these values should always receive top priority. The point is rather that the three may often be in tension and yet all are likely to be important to the overall legitimacy of the policy process. *Legitimacy* refers to the general satisfaction of citizens and other political actors (such as elected officials, constituency groups, and organizational members) with policy making. Here, we pay most attention to *procedural* or *process* legitimacy, focusing upon *how* decisions are made rather than what decisions ultimately result (though legitimacy will inevitably have substantive components as well). In this view, actors treat decision outcomes as authoritative—even if they disagree with the policy content—when policies are formulated in acceptable ways, through justifiable procedures. What constitutes "acceptable" ways of formulating policy may reflect the perceived rationality, representativeness, or accountability of policy making.

In the United States, the apparent requirements for "process legitimacy" have changed over time. Richard Stewart (1975) traces the development of normative views of bureaucratic decision making. In the late nineteenth and early twentieth centuries, "politics" and "administration" defined sharply delimited spheres. U.S. government agencies were to be nothing more than "transmission belts" for attaining the directives of elected officials, and accountability to the demands of these officials was paramount. By the time of the New Deal, though, the view of government as a haven for venerated technical "experts" became more accepted, and "bureaucratic rationality" rose to the fore. In the 1960s, the battle cries of those demanding desegregation, U.S. withdrawal from Vietnam, community control of public schools, and tougher environmental protection laws blended into pressures for greater citizen participation in policy making and thus for greater representativeness in administrative agencies. Today our expectations of government organizations seem to encompass accountability, bureaucratic rationality, and representativeness, all at once:

An adequate administrative decision process must produce a "reasonable decision" and convince the public that a responsible and rational determination has been made. This presupposes the opportunity for appropriate substantive comment by the public and a mechanism of . . . response that indicates convincingly that these comments have been considered fairly and adequately in reaching the decision. (Whitney, 1976, pp. 51–52)

The exact mix of process values necessary for legitimacy probably varies at least in part with the problem setting. When goals are controversial, for example, a premium may be placed on the representation of differing viewpoints and on organizational accountability. As much of the outcry over the Iran-contra situation indicated, when neither the public nor elected officials can agree on policy objectives, efforts by unelected officials to articulate and pursue policy goals likely will meet with firm resistance. High technical and goal uncertainty may point to the need for governance structures that are closely tied to elected officials who have greater recognized responsibility for making "tough" decisions, as well as for structures that grant access to representatives of diverse viewpoints to help officials explore their options. One likely constant, however, is that agency officials will devote considerable effort to ensuring that their decision processes are seen as legitimate by relevant outsiders (cf. DiMaggio & Powell, 1983; Pfeffer & Salancik, 1978, p. 102; J. Thompson, 1967, p. 88).

Different governance structures incorporate varying notions and mixes of the four process values. Table 2 returns to the structures introduced in chapter 3 and suggests what the values might mean in the context of each of the structures.

Process Values Reconsidered

Not everyone agrees with an understanding of appropriate decision making that stresses process values. William Gormley, for instance, contends that substantive as well as procedural values are critical to institutional redesign and that analysts typically underemphasize substantive values (1987, pp. 155–57). Yet even he notes that "as issues become more technical and more complex, substantive policy outcomes become more difficult to determine or predict. Under such circumstances, the cultivation of shared procedural values helps to ensure public confidence and elite support in the face of technical uncertainty" (1987, p. 156).

Thomas O. McGarity goes further. "Because science policy questions are scientifically unresolvable at the time a decision must be made, it is not illogical or inappropriate for politicians to urge the regulators to resolve them in a way that will reach a particular result" (1979, p. 782). As understandable as this counsel may be, however, it assumes a consensus about goals; it also offers little guidance to officials actively wrestling with technical uncertainty or controversy.

More generally, we do not believe that focusing on decision processes means completely ignoring decision substance (cf. Yates, 1982, p. 172).

TABLE 2 Process Values and Governance Structures

	Governance Structure			
	Hierarchical	Adjudicative	Adversarial	Market
Bureaucratic rationality Problem definition/ interpretation	Congruence with standard procedures	Two opposed views, one of which is "correct"	Multifaceted, conflicting perspectives	Ill-structured, beyond human comprehension or control
Ability to reach closure	High, if responsible decision maker is willing to decide or rules dictate outcomes	High: third party decides	High, if uninvolved decision maker acts	Indeterminate: decisions "emerge"
Accountability	High to top official, external overseers	High, given clear standards on which "judge" is to base decision	High to constituencies, clientele groups; lower to overseers	Low direct accountability
Representativeness	Less variety, diversity than in other structures (Stout, 1980)	Rights of participants, occupants of polar positions	All defined as "parties"	"Status quo" interests advantaged (Bryson, 1984)
Primary sources of legitimacy	Efficiency, accountability	Fairness of procedure (Yellin, 1983, p. 1312)	Openness, fullness of debate	"Freedom," efficiency

(continued)

TABLE 2 *(continued)*

	Governance Structure		
	Collegial-Competitive	Collegial-Consensual	Collegial-Mediative
Bureaucratic rationality			
Problem definition/interpretation	Multifaceted; existence of common ground, possibility of compromise	Collective search necessary for appropriate response; problem affects shared interests	Conflicting perspectives; common ground possible
Ability to reach closure	High: formal voting rules in absence of consensus; closure may be temporary as issues become polarized, more "redistributive" (Ripley & Franklin, 1984)	High, if common interests can be discovered (Mansbridge, 1980); low, if conflict is polarizing or "redistributive" (Rothschild-Whitt, 1979)	High, given mediator skill and perceptions of shared interests
Accountability	Moderate to constituencies/clients: negotiation may produce decisions desired by few	May be very low; "discovery," developing consensus are higher priorities	Moderate to constituents/clients
Representativeness	All "interested parties"	Potentially wide, not highly salient: premium placed on ability/willingness to explore options, work toward consensus	All defined as "parties"
Primary sources of legitimacy	Representativeness; fairness and openness of process	Openness, equality of participation, representativeness	Fullness of hearing, acceptability of mediator

Consideration of bureaucratic rationality most explicitly introduces policy content into assessments of decision making, for it highlights the range and quality of information, analysis, and evaluation included in the process. Similarly, representativeness taps the extent to which those with differing "substantive values"—for example, social equity, equality, or family stability (Gormley, 1987, p. 156)—are meaningfully included in decision making.

In a representative democracy, accountability to elected officials also draws attention to policy content, at least to the extent that elected officials or their agents provide some substantive direction to agencies or accept their acknowledged responsibility for being involved in decisions made under conditions of uncertainty or controversy. In addition, accountability, as we have defined it, seems able to encompass Douglas Yates's insistence that agency officials give a "public accounting" of their decision making when it involves "a nonroutine new initiative . . . , a marked departure from past practice . . . , [or] the application of major social values such as equality, equal opportunity, personal liberty . . . " (1982, p. 176). Finally, citizens and other political actors often will judge the legitimacy of policy decisions in part by their outcomes.

These observations do not imply that analysts should never use substantive values to guide normative inquiry. However, when inquiring into the appropriate mechanisms for organizational decision making, they should concentrate on designing structures that heighten the probability that desired ends and means will be selected and pursued. In what is, at least in principle, a representative democracy like the United States, that means both that the design must permit legitimate actors to advocate their preferred goals and policy strategies, and that those decision makers are able to make legitimate decisions (and non-decisions) when there is uncertainty or controversy.

Coping with Uncertainty and Controversy

The four process values are the foundation for our conception of appropriate structuring. They also provide the basis for several, more fine-grained assumptions about how organizations should cope with uncertainty, controversy, and certainty or consensus.

First, coping with *uncertainty* requires that organizations search for information and diverse judgments. Such mobilization of expertise may not eliminate uncertainty, but it may reduce it or render it more manageable. Second, in the long run, organizations best handle *controversy* by bringing together representatives of contending parties and viewpoints (see, e.g., Burke, 1986, p. 145; Lindblom, 1959; Schweiger, Sandberg, & Ragan, 1986). Open discussion or debate aims, then, at finding a solution or at least a satisfactory "quasi-resolution" (Cyert & March, 1963) of the differences. Third, when one element of a problem is controversial and the other uncertain, structures should focus primarily on the area of controversy.

Handling the conflict will, in effect, incorporate a decision about how to cope with the uncertainty—a line of reasoning similar to that of Lindblom (1959), who recommends selecting means and ends simultaneously.

Note that under conditions of either uncertainty or controversy, these premises stress the importance of structures that permit the gathering of a wide range of information and interpretations, thus enhancing bureaucratic rationality. Representativeness is also sought: agencies are urged to search for advocates with diverse views. Accountability can be obtained through both initial design and participation by citizens and elected officials or their agents in actual decision making.

Fourth, and finally, in a situation of *goal consensus* and *technical certainty*, Weberian hierarchy is most appropriate. Representativeness becomes less important, since interested parties agree upon ends and means. In principle, at least, classical hierarchy generally helps ensure both bureaucratic rationality and accountability (through what is often called "overhead democracy"; see Redford, 1969).

LINKING STRUCTURE AND DECISION SETTING

The key question remains: what type of governance structure is most appropriate for which problem setting? Table 3 summarizes the major elements of our answer. We are following what might be called a *problem contingency* approach: our analysis is based on the assumption that governance structures should vary with the problem settings in which they are embedded (see Gruber, 1987, ch. 5, for another example of such an approach).

Before we discuss each of the cells in the table, two cautions must be repeated. First, at this stage, our analysis is explicitly *prescriptive*. Whether table 3 has predictive or explanatory capacity is an issue we will take up in chapter 6. Second, recall that characterizations of the problem setting—for example, as having technical controversy and goal consensus—refer to the *internal* organizational milieu. Moreover, they need not hold for an agency as a whole, but rather only for particular decision settings.

Cell 1: Inspiration and Market Structures

Situations in which decision makers know neither what to do nor how to do it may be more common than one might suspect. "Inspiration" (J. Thompson, 1967) refers to processes, whether individual or collective, for selecting purposes and at least experimenting with ways of attaining them. In group contexts, what may be required is what James MacGregor Burns calls "transforming leadership." Such leadership emerges:

TABLE 3   Decision Settings and Appropriate Governance Structure

Technologies (State of Beliefs About Causation)	Goals (State of Preferences About Possible Outcomes)		
	Uncertainty	Consensus	Controversy
Uncertainty	**1** Inspiration/ Market ("Transforming" leadership or structure allowing decisions to emerge)	**2** Collegial-Consensual (Consensus-seeking, collaboration)	**3** Collegial-Competitive/ Collegial-Mediative (Representation of experts and stakeholders; formal decision rules)
Certainty	**4** Collegial-Consensual ("Brainstorming" techniques: Delphi, Nominal Group)	**5** Hierarchical (Programmed decision authority)	**6** Collegial-Competitive/ Collegial-Mediative (Stakeholder representation; formal decision rules)
Controversy	**7** Adversarial (Multiparty advocacy, with judgment by disinterested party; some concern for stakeholder and expert representation)	**8** Adjudicative (Formal rules of argumentation and decision, with judgment by disinterested party)	**9** Indeterminate (Structure must be perceived as legitimate; either hierarchy or structure facilitating representation is likely)

when one or more persons *engage* with others in such a way that leaders and followers raise one another to higher levels of motivation and morality . . . [Transforming leadership] raises the level of human conduct and ethical aspiration of both leaders and led. (1978, p. 20; Burns's emphasis)

Transforming leadership may promote a redefinition of goals or cause followers to rally around a particular policy option, moving the decision problem out of cell 1 altogether. Franklin Roosevelt's ability to galvanize subordinates and citizens alike owed much to his skills of transforming leadership; many found the same talent behind Oliver North's temporary mobilization of popular support for U.S. military aid to the Nicaraguan contras.

Alternatively, decision making may be left to more market-like structures. Perhaps as presidents realize the many limitations of their office, they come to rely on these structures in some policy arenas, allowing decisions to "emerge," with the president receiving scant blame or credit. Jimmy Carter's experimentation with "spontaneous and self-monitoring Cabinet government" (Campbell, 1986, p. 216) suggests, however, that this "hands-off" posture may be difficult to sustain and to legitimize. Carter found it hard to restrain himself from delving into operational detail, and the perception of cabinet members as working at cross-purposes led many to accuse the White House of incompetence and lack of leadership.

Cells 2 and 4: Collegial-Consensual Structures

When goals are not in doubt but technologies are uncertain (cell 2), organizations should engage in search behavior that attempts to identify possible technical responses and their potential consequences. Indicated are collegial-consensual structures that encourage collaboration among experts. Thus, Rosabeth Moss Kanter recommends the use of teams in private firms as a means of gaining "new sources of expertise and experience" and allowing "more wide-ranging or creative discussions and solutions" (1983, pp. 242–43). Proponents of the establishment of committees of scientists, engineers, and lawyers to act as "standing masters" in complex environmental cases seem to have similar objectives (e.g., Yellin, 1981, pp. 555–56). Within the Food and Drug Administration, the Bureau of Drugs Office creates teams of experts to evaluate new drug applications. Members typically include a medical officer to evaluate data from clinical tests, a pharmacist responsible for assessing animal tests, chemists to review the chemical and manufacturing processes, and, occasionally, a statistician or microbiologist (Bryner, 1987, p. 195). In this instance, the goal is clear and agreed-upon (only safe drugs should be approved for use by the general public), while the means of establishing that a drug is "safe" are more ambiguous. If technical agreement fails to occur in such collegial-consensual structures, however, decision making may shift into cell 8.

Collegial-consensual structures also appear to be appropriate when technology is not problematical but goals are ill-defined (cell 4). Here, such structures channel efforts to arrive at some workable agreement concerning the direction or directions in which policy should move. Needed are mechanisms that permit the free exchange of ideas, as well as decision rules and norms that stress the development of consensus and promote collaboration. Participants will likely include both generalists and experts, all committed to examining past interpretations of policy goals and to searching for new formulations.

The private sector has developed a repertoire of methods for helping organizations cope with such situations—for example, structured brainstorming sessions such as those introduced by the Nominal Group and

Delphi techniques. These are used less often in the public sector, although local governments have experimented with several of them (see, e.g., Mahler, 1987). When Jimmy Carter retreated with trusted advisers to Camp David to rethink the direction of his administration, he evidently was attempting to fashion a process of cooperative search.

Cells 3 and 6: Collegial-Competitive and Collegial-Mediative Structures

When goals are controversial, actors need to engage in some sort of give-and-take, or negotiation. Required are governance structures that facilitate the airing and acceptable weighting of various points of view and that provide decision rules for closing debate in the absence of consensus (cf. Ingraham, 1987, p. 621). Collegial-competitive structures have some of the properties associated with legislative bodies—collegiality, representation, discussion of and bargaining over conflicting views, and voting rules. Collegial-mediative structures offer similar arenas for discussion and negotiation while providing a mediator to help competing sides clarify their differences or search for common ground (e.g., Ozawa & Susskind, 1985, pp. 31–34). Since the outcomes produced by both structures may depend upon the support of participants and outside observers, representation according to some agreed-upon principle is essential for legitimacy. When technical uncertainty is present (cell 3), some provision for permitting experts to be included or to play a role—for example, as staff or as "proxy advocates"—is apt to be desirable.

Government organizations tend to be rife with collegial-competitive structures. For example, considerable controversy swirls over the objectives of, and possible limits to, biomedical research; available technologies raise a host of uncertainties. One of the ways the National Institutes of Health (NIH) have responded to what appears to be a cell 3 setting is by establishing the National Advisory Commission for the Protection of Human Subjects of Biomedical Research. The commission includes both scientists and laypeople, in an effort to represent a spectrum of expert and "public" concerns (Nelkin, 1984, p. 21).

Presidency scholar Colin Campbell praises another collegial-competitive structure, the National Security Council under Dwight Eisenhower. The NSC "got competing interests talking at an early stage," allowed the identification of contentious points and possible agreements, and ended debate by either reaching a negotiated conclusion or sending split decisions to the president (1986, p. 51). U.S. foreign policy making continues to rely on collegial-competitive arrangements. The National Foreign Intelligence Board, for example, brings together the directors of all U.S. intelligence agencies (such as the CIA, National Security Agency, Defense Intelligence Agency, and foreign intelligence units in the State Department and FBI) to share information and thrash out differences (see, e.g., Woodward, 1987).

As chapter 3 suggested, collegial-mediative structures are less common. In April 1985, however, the Environmental Protection Agency experimented with mediation in drafting new rules on emergency exemptions for pesticide restrictions under the Federal Insecticide, Fungicide, and Rodenticide Act (Kettl, 1988, pp. 134–37). Goals were highly controversial: for example, environmentalists emphasized the danger of pesticides to humans and the physical environment; manufacturers and processors were concerned with both the economic implications of the restrictions and possible liability issues; growers stressed the importance of pesticides in protecting their crop yields. Meanwhile, the techniques for determining the effects of pesticides and the means of implementing the exemptions were uncertain. EPA official LaJuana Wilcher (who had had no previous involvement with pesticide regulation) served as a mediator working with twenty-two interested parties to develop the proposed regulations. The group succeeded in publishing the proposed rules, which received only nineteen comments (most on minor issues) and were finalized without court challenge.

Cell 5: Hierarchical Structures

When ends and means are certain, as we argued earlier, decision making becomes a "technical or mechanical matter" (J. Thompson & Tuden, 1959, p. 198). Decision making can, in principle, be fully programmed, and thus hierarchy is appropriate. Much of the day-to-day work of government agencies—processing tax returns, sending out Social Security checks, collecting trash—can be handled quite efficiently and effectively through routines and standard operating procedures. Indeed, Charles Perrow (1986, ch. 1) contends that many complaints about government service reflect the need for stricter or more vigorously enforced rules; in some cases, we may need *more* hierarchy, not less. Meanwhile, as we have seen, hierarchy is an overriding organizational principle in government for another, quite potent reason: it allegedly fosters accountability.

Cell 7: Adversarial Structures

When controversy erupts over technology and goals are uncertain, efforts should be directed both at trying to reduce conflict by exploring disputed points of view and at avoiding capture of the decision making by experts. Alvin Weinberg believes that adversarial structures are particularly useful for handling "trans-scientific" questions, for the structures illuminate key assumptions and disagreements (1979, p. 215). Adversarial structures pit those who disagree about technology against one another while leaving the final decision to another party. Since goals are uncertain, to preserve accountability the deciding party should probably be elected officials, political appointees, or their delegates.

President Reagan, for example, had a habit of seeking "advice directly from individuals, even if it's in the context of a meeting in which strong people are disagreeing violently with each other" (R. Porter, 1985, p. 37). Dwight Eisenhower, the alleged proponent of formalistic, hierarchical structures, sometimes relied upon adversarial mechanisms as a means of exploring diverse policy options. His 1953 "solarium study" charged three study groups—each with differing interpretations of the objectives, actions, and policies of the Soviet Union—with evaluating U.S. policy toward the U.S.S.R. (Kernell & Popkin, 1986, p. 119).

Agencies as well as presidents may benefit from adversarial approaches. For instance, some critics argue that agency rule making relies too heavily on evidence and arguments submitted by outside "experts," a tendency the courts may reinforce by requiring a growing range of judicial procedures in gathering and considering public input. As a consequence, decision making can drag on almost interminably, and agency officials sometimes have little real influence over the final decisions, being reduced instead to following the "preponderance" of the evidence. In effect, representativeness may be overemphasized, while bureaucratic rationality and accountability are neglected. In such circumstances, more adversarial structuring may be called for. Eisenberg, for example, proposes an alternative kind of decision making: the "consultative process" view. Agency decision makers would be required to solicit and consider input, but they would no longer be bound by the "norm of strong responsiveness":

> [T]he decision need not proceed from or be congruent with the parties' proofs and arguments. Instead the decision-maker may base his [sic] decision solely on evidence he has himself collected, on his experience, on his institutional preferences, and on rules neither adduced nor addressed by the parties. (Eisenberg, 1978, p. 414)

Cell 8: Adjudicative Structures

Here, as in cell 7, advocates seek to convince an uncommitted decision maker of the validity of their technical claims. Since goals are agreed upon, adjudicative structures become appropriate, with the relevant values determining the burden of proof. Thus, proposals for science courts typically assume that "scientific" (that is, technical) questions can be separated from issues regarding "values"; the courts would address only the former (e.g., Martin, 1979, p. 447).

In "pure" adjudicative structures, the decision maker or "judge" is largely passive, assessing the parties' arguments against the burden of proof rather than trying to cope directly with technical controversy. Accountability flows from acting within the bounds of specified goals, not from having publicly answerable officials making (or overseeing) the decision. Recall as well that adjudicative structures tend to treat disputes as having only two sides, with outcomes cast as winning or losing.

Regulatory agencies rely heavily on mechanisms growing out of adjudicative models, developing rules of evidence and restrictions on decision makers' communication with outside parties patterned after those of courts (e.g., Schuck, 1979, p. 27). Not surprisingly, adjudicative structures have special legitimacy in the U.S. political system, with its grounding in Anglo-American jurisprudence.

Cell 9: Indeterminate

Decision making becomes particularly difficult when both goals and technologies are in dispute. The number of dimensions of disagreement may make negotiation unworkable. Even majority voting solutions may be elusive, since coalitions may be hard to form or to keep stable. In cases where any decision will provoke widespread opposition, the overriding requirement is that the decision process be perceived as legitimate. In general, no particular structure seems more appropriate than any other. As our discussion thus far has hinted, though, the American political culture seems to regard some governance structures as especially legitimate—for example, hierarchy (with its emphasis on accountability through overhead democracy), collegial-competitive structures resembling legislatures (which seem to promise representativeness), and adjudicative structures (providing accountability in the guise of the "rule of law").

In the White House, for instance, we expect the buck to reach, and to stop with, the president. When it does not, as in the Iran-contra affair, legitimacy becomes the key issue. NASA responded to the *Challenger* explosion in part by increasing the amount of rules and hierarchy, thus reining in expert discretion (Romzek & Dubnick, 1987). This arguably is a way for top agency administrators to appear to be taking control, by pursuing bureaucratic rationality and accountability, and hence legitimacy.

SYSTEM EFFECTS

Different decision settings seem to call for different governance structures. As we have stressed, however, at this stage it is unclear whether actual organizations rely on the structures that table 3 indicates are most appropriate. Chapter 6 explores that issue further.

Before we move on, though, we should stress that structure is more than a "dependent variable": it influences whether and how policy issues are recognized, and it helps shape the bureaucratic rationality, representativeness, accountability, and legitimacy of decision making.

Governance structures also have broader, more diffuse impacts on organizations that affect their political systems. Table 4 summarizes illustrative "system effects" for the structures we have discussed.

First, governance structures help define what is meant by "leadership" in particular decision settings. In hierarchies, for example, we often associate leadership with holding the top position. In adversarial structures, leadership is more apt to be seen in those who can probe for weaknesses in others' arguments or persuade the final decision maker that particular paths should be followed.

Second, structures may affect internal configurations of power. Collegial-consensual mechanisms may spread power among several relatively equal collaborators; alternatively, cooperation may flow from the presence of a single authoritative figure who demands it. In market structures, power is likely to be dispersed; how equally influence is shared probably will vary, just as it does in economic markets.

Third, governance structures may offer hints at how much change is likely to be attainable as a result of their operation (cf. Braybrooke & Lindblom, 1963, p. 78). Adjudicative mechanisms, for instance, may produce a high degree of change if the "winning" side proposes a major departure from current practice (as happened, for example, with the *Brown v. Board of Education* decision outlawing segregated schools). If decision makers follow "precedent," however, very little change may occur. Less clear are the effects of the three types of collegial structure. They may be more likely to trigger major shifts if broader search processes yield numerous options and wide-ranging evaluation. Yet the need to reach consensus or agree to a compromise, and in some cases to work together again in the future, may reduce the chances of large-scale change. This may be especially true in collegial-competitive structures if decision makers become wary of the negative effect of strong, overt disagreement on the future stability and predictability of decision outcomes (Walcott, 1971).

In summary, a problem contingency approach to organizational design highlights the importance of adapting structures to prevailing decision settings. Selecting appropriate structures, we have argued, can enhance the bureaucratic rationality, accountability, representativeness, and legitimacy of public policy making. In turn, governance structures may shape the nature of organizational politics.

Do actual organizations rely on governance structures that reflect their problem environments? We turn next to that question.

TABLE 4 Some Effects of Governance Structures in Organizational Political Systems

	Governance Structure			
	Hierarchical	Adjudicative	Adversarial	Market
Definition of leadership	Occupancy of superordinate position	Ability to shape arguments, marshal evidence, persuade judge, establish burden of proof	Ability to probe for weaknesses in arguments, find points of agreement	Initial design of "market"
Internal configuration of power	Influence flows from top down	Influence flows to those able to set value/issue agenda, those with persuasive skills	Power diffused to subunits, centers of advocacy	Varies from dispersed to concentrated
Degree of change promoted	Very high (Bryson, 1984; Ouchi, 1980) or very low (Browne & Wildavsky, 1984)	Very high or very low	Moderate, incremental	Low; tends toward "equilibrium"

(continued)

TABLE 4 *(continued)*

	Governance Structure			
	Collegial-Competitive	Collegial-Consensual	Collegial-Mediative	
Definition of leadership	Ability to guide discussion, bargaining	Skill at discovering and promoting consensus	Ability to mobilize parties to seek areas of shared interest and consider settlements	
Internal configuration of power	Diffused: influence flows to those with stronger bargaining positions, skills	Influence dispersed or highly concentrated	Influence distributed among parties, may concentrate in those with least stake in settlement or access to alternative decision mechanisms	
Degree of change promoted	Unclear: lower, reflecting compromise, *or* higher, since structure may promote search and change (Browne & Wildavsky, 1984); higher "consolidative" change (reducing internal stress), but lower "adaptive" change (responding to the environment) (Davidson & Olezsek, 1976)	Unclear: higher insofar as structure encourages broad search and consideration of numerous options; lower given consensus requirement	Moderate, reflecting compromise	

CHAPTER SIX

The Real World of Organizations

Thus far, our discussion has been primarily normative in tone. The last chapter offered prescriptions for potentially appropriate structures, but can it help us understand what actually goes on in the depths of government organizations? What kinds of governance structures currently exist, and why? Is there a pressing need to change the way public agencies make decisions?

Our answers—like the "dense complexity" of organization itself—are rather complicated. Some governance structures evidently do "match" their decision settings in the way table 3 might predict. At the same time, the organizational landscape is littered with apparent "mismatches." Examining why these fits and misfits occur should deepen our understanding of the structuring and dynamics of government organizations and also point to some of the empirical uses of the governance model.

FITS AND MISFITS: EXISTING GOVERNANCE STRUCTURES

Unfortunately, there are no systematic surveys of the types of structures found in government organizations. Nevertheless, anecdotal evidence suggests that the range of governance structures is wide.

Some appear to match the prescriptions contained in table 3 (see page 72). As we have mentioned, collegial-competitive structures are fairly common, perhaps because of the legitimacy accorded legislative mechanisms in the United States. For example, the 1982 Nuclear Waste Policy Act gave the Department of Energy (DOE) considerable discretion in negotiating with and compensating states and localities that accept nuclear waste storage facilities. In the past, disputes over the siting of such operations frequently were settled in court. The 1982 decision was a key innovation—a shift from "adjudication" (cell 8 in table 3) to "negotiation" (cell 3) (Sigmon, 1987, p. 171; cf. Downey, 1985). Decisions about locating nuclear waste operations seem to be characterized by goal controversy and technical uncertainty. DOE, acting on behalf of the nation as a whole, is concerned with disposing nuclear wastes; those near potential storage sites are likely to worry more about health and safety risks and about the possible negative effects of nuclear waste facilities on economic development and tourism. Meanwhile, the available technologies for transporting, handling, and storing wastes pose considerable uncertainty.

Even here, however, negotiation is not a sure-fire strategy. In Tennessee, while Roane County and the city of Oak Ridge agreed to enter into negotiations over siting a "monitored retrievable storage" facility, both the state of Tennessee and another potential site, Hartsville, refused. The issue ended up in court, where the state lost its bid to block DOE from recommending a site in Tennessee to Congress (McCabe & Fitzgerald, 1987). Without greater incentives for all interested parties to come to (and stay at) the bargaining table, collegial-competitive structures may fail (Sigmon, 1987, p. 177).

Evidently more successful are the required conferences between officials of the Mine Safety and Health Administration (MSHA) and mine operators, which now take place before MSHA issues citations for alleged violations. Former Assistant Secretary of Labor Ford B. Ford initiated these meetings, where changes in mining procedures are mapped out, after he grew concerned with the "confrontational nature" of the enforcement of the Mine Safety and Health Act (Lynn, 1984, p. 350). The conferences seem to be an appropriate response to a setting marked by competing goals and safety technologies with uncertain effects. Apparently, they have transformed mine inspectors from "enforcers of rules" into "agents for safety" (Lynn, 1984, p. 364). Although organized labor and some agency officials worry that the reform may compromise mine safety (Lynn, 1984, p. 366), the implication may be that the interests represented at the conferences need to be expanded rather than that the structure itself should be abandoned. Whether such a change would lead to different policy outcomes is unclear, but it probably would enhance the legitimacy of the decision process.

Public organizations also rely on other governance structures that we have discussed. For example, Harvey Sapolsky analyzed the development of the Polaris missile system—a "successful" program that deployed the fleet ballistic missile system (FBM) ahead of schedule, with no cost overruns. Even rarer these days, the system worked (1972, p. 11). Among the reasons for the success, according to Sapolsky, was the adversarial structure that pitted Navy and Air Force officials against one another, with final decisions on weapon system deployment made by higher-ups in the Pentagon.

> [This] forced both services to examine carefully the missiles and the operational doctrines that they were developing. For example, the [Navy's] Special Projects Office's plan for two crews to increase the on-station time of FBM submarines can be attributed to Air Force criticism that, with normal overhauls and crew schedules, it would take three Polaris submarines to keep one within range of Soviet targets. Also the strategic value of the FBM system's vulnerability was not well appreciated until the Air Force argued strongly the comparative cost advantages of land-based missiles. (Sapolsky, 1972, pp. 40–41)

Many more examples of matches between decision settings and actual structures could be cited. Evident mismatches, however, also are abundant. For example, much recent criticism has focused on the use of adjudicative structures, particularly in formal agency rule making and in reliance on the courts to settle disputes. Too often, these structures are used when goal consensus is lacking. Yellin argues that in controversies over the siting of nuclear power plants the tendency of adjudicative structures to reduce debates to two sides and to emphasize winning detracts from the bureaucratic rationality of the decisions. Rationality suffers because the structures provide few incentives for the parties to fully explore competing goals, such as conserving energy versus increasing production or protecting the environment versus fostering economic development (Yellin, 1981, p. 508; cf. Bryner, 1987, p. 204).

Similarly, West (1985) criticizes the Federal Trade Commission's use of "judicialized procedures." According to the Magnuson-Moss Act, the FTC must base its rules on evidence presented in adjudicative proceedings. Such a requirement assumes that "legislative goals are clearly discernable and that agency actions should therefore be evaluated objectively in terms of set criteria" (West, 1985, p. 172). Even though goals often conflict and technologies are ambiguous or controversial, agency expertise is, in effect, "irrelevant." The commission cannot "rely on its own informed judgment in dealing with 'polycentric' policy problems, the complexity of which precludes tight, empirically justifiable solutions" (West, 1985, p. 172). Meanwhile, adjudicative structuring has encouraged participants to assume confrontational postures and limited FTC's ability to forge compromises among competing interests (West, 1985, pp. 11, 173). Both bureaucratic rationality and meaningful representation are thus stunted as well. In such instances, reliance upon adjudicative structures probably also has increased public skepticism about the legitimacy of the decision process (Yellin, 1983, p. 1332; cf. Brett & Goldberg, 1983; Greenwood, 1984; Kimm, Kuzmack, & Schnare, 1981, p. 243).

These settings are all characterized by goal controversy and technical uncertainty and evidently call for more collegial-competitive governance structures (cell 3). Such mechanisms foster negotiation, which:

lays bare all the uncertainties and complexities . . . As the parties dissect their points of disagreement, they are forced to confront the elusive nature of facts . . . Moreover, the parties may be forced to compromise on matters of principle. The pulling and hauling that is the essence of bargaining forces the parties to recognize that there are no right answers—only compromise . . . Instead of creating the illusion of truth, bargaining embraces the accommodation of competing interests. (Bacow & Wheeler, 1984, p. 364)

Other governance structures also seem to be used in inappropriate settings. Mahler (1987) reports, for instance, on the dissatisfaction of some participants with the use of a collegial-consensual strategy, the Nominal Group Technique,[1] in public sector decision making. Critically, in many of the settings she studied (for example, policy making by a regional transportation commission), the technique was used to address deep-seated value conflicts rather than to help decision makers probe genuine uncertainty. Structures appropriate for cells 2 and 4 were used in situations that more closely resembled those described by cell 3.

ACCOUNTING FOR EXISTING GOVERNANCE STRUCTURES

Once matches and mismatches between the prescriptions in table 3 and actual decision structures have been identified, more difficult questions arise: What is the evident balance between "appropriate" and "inappropriate" structures in government? And why do certain structures emerge and persist? Without an inventory of extant structures, the first question cannot be answered definitively. We will maintain, though, that, for several reasons, governance structures vary far less than the analysis in previous chapters might lead one to expect. In particular, hierarchy appears to be the dominant structural form. Not only is it the overall, or "meta," structure for most government agencies, but its principles are commonly employed in these organizations as the preferred mode of decision making.

Clearly, however, there are many nonhierarchical structures and numerous catalysts of organizational innovation. One such catalyst is simply dissatisfaction with the performance of conventional hierarchies. Unhappy with the risk-averse, overgeneralized analyses he received through normal channels at the State Department, for example, President Kennedy soon

---

1 According to Julianne G. Mahler, Nominal Group Technique aims at "arriving at creative, nonroutine decisions" through "nonconflictual" means (1987, p. 337). She describes the process as it was used by several local public decision makers: "(1) individuals independently list possible alternative goals or solutions to a problem, (2) each alternative is presented in turn around the group until each person has exhausted his or her list, (3) any alternative may be clarified, but no lobbying for or against an alternative is allowed, (4) each participant independently ranks the set of alternatives, and (5) the priority of the alternatives is established through some form of voting or mathematical pooling of individual rankings" (1987, p. 337). Brainstorming often precedes these steps (cf. Delbecq, Van de Ven, & Gustavson, 1975).

made it a habit to consult directly with lower-level officials, who often provided more substantive and varied perspectives. At other times, external actors may dictate that agencies use particular alternative structures. As we have noted, the courts have imposed a range of decision structures on agencies, just as the Nuclear Waste Policy Act introduced the Department of Energy to negotiation. In addition, organizational fads often float between agencies, across levels of government, and from the private to the public sector. Citizen and expert advisory panels multiplied for a time in the sixties and early seventies, while management journals, consultants, and private sector officials entering government urged use of the Delphi technique and management retreats.

Not all these innovations, of course, are likely to be appropriate. Indeed, overall, we suggest that "inappropriate" governance structures probably outnumber "appropriate" ones. Most critically, we will contend, hierarchy often prevails under conditions of uncertainty or controversy, when it may well be inappropriate. Moreover, as chapter 7 will elaborate, nonhierarchical governance structures frequently are embedded in larger authoritarian, "bureaucratic" processes (or governance "networks").

If one accepts the plausibility of the hypothesized links between decision type and governance structure, how can we account for evident mismatches? Part of the explanation lies in the slipperiness of the notion of appropriateness. In particular, policy makers' views of "appropriate" structures may differ dramatically from the emphases we have outlined. Much depends upon which criteria of appropriateness are employed. For example, in the U.S. political system, concern with protecting individual rights may outweigh other values, leading to reliance on adjudicative structures and judicial resolution of political and technical conflicts. Similarly, distrust of agency officials may foster insistence on hierarchically induced accountability. John Chubb (1988) argues, for example, that the perceived failures of American public schools have triggered a vicious circle. A growing body of data suggests that making schools more autonomous and organizing them internally as nonhierarchical "teams" contributes to improved student performance. Yet, evidence of poor performance typically provokes calls for stricter hierarchy and greater control by outsiders such as central administration and state education departments. Implementing such prescriptions may in turn cause further deterioration, leading to even more demands for greater external supervision.

Moreover, as we suggested at the outset, the values contributing to appropriateness may themselves conflict, producing difficult tradeoffs. While some complain bitterly about the ways in which hierarchy weakens clients and employees alike (e.g., Ferguson, 1984; Perrow, 1986), others contend that hierarchy must lie at the basis of any effort to achieve bureaucratic rationality (e.g., Mashaw, 1983). When some controversy exists, research (e.g., Schweiger, Sandberg, & Ragan, 1986, pp. 66–68) suggests that decision structures that air the conflicts (such as the structures in cells 3, 6,

7, and 8) generate higher-quality strategic decisions. In other words, they may heighten bureaucratic rationality. Yet, in the same situations, structures that aim at producing consensus lead to greater participant satisfaction and more of a desire to work together in the future; consensual structures may seem to members to be more legitimate. This does not mean that bureaucratic rationality is completely ignored: policies fashioned in consensual structures also tend to be more readily implemented. Thus, decision makers might well opt for more consensual structures, especially if participant satisfaction is important for ongoing support.

Another reason for apparent differences between prescribed and actual structures flows from the nature of the problem settings organizations confront. Our concepts of goal and technical consensus/certainty, uncertainty, and controversy have both objective and subjective components. On the one hand, they tap the "objective"[2] circumstances characterizing particular decision settings; as we argued in chapter 4, goal consensus and understanding of cause-effect relationships vary considerably across decision arenas. On the other hand, *perceptions* of decision settings play an important mediating role; as Dery observes, "problems do not come with a tag identifying them" (1984, p. 62; cf. Douglas & Wildavsky, 1982). In the most immediate sense, a problem *is* whatever the relevant decision makers define it to be. Especially when problems are vague or multifaceted, this accords a great deal of discretion to decision makers. Moreover, in disputes involving both technical and goal controversy or uncertainty, there may be a "definitional bias":

> Too often, highly political issues are defined as technical; questions about the impact of a technology on community values are translated into arguments about the degree of risk involved. It is somehow assumed that agreement about technical issues will help resolve questions of political choice. (Nelkin & Pollak, 1980, p. 271)

Perceptions of problem settings are shaped by a variety of factors in addition to the "objective" uncertainty or controversy. For instance, a unit's permeability, or openness, to its environment is likely to affect its understanding of the decision setting. One can observe this factor at work at the very top of the executive branch. As aides to Herbert Hoover and Richard Nixon erected increasingly secure "protective" walls around the White House, neither president, even had he been so inclined, had much opportunity to get a sense of the tumult outside Washington. The growing isolation of the presidents may be explained by the fact that both staffs were designed for situations of greater consensus and certainty (on Hoover, see, e.g., Walcott & Hult, forthcoming; on Nixon, e.g., Rather & Gates, 1974).

The distribution and dynamics of power within an organization also can influence how problems are defined. Recall that in the parental notification case there seemed to be both goal controversy and technical uncertainty; under such conditions, table 3 would prescribe use of

---

2 Dror, however, argues against employing the term "objective" (1986, p. 20).

collegial-competitive or collegial-mediative structures (cell 3). What developed instead were hierarchical decision making directed by political appointees (cell 5) and an informal collegial-competitive structure that excluded technical experts (cell 6); over time, the latter took on an adjudicative character (moving to cell 8) as participants prepared to defend the final rule in court. Part of the explanation can be found in the changing patterns of power within the Department of Health and Human Services (DHHS). Power flowed to political executives and lawyers. The former traded on their links to a White House that was very interested in reshaping administrative rule making (see, e.g., Nathan, 1983) and responding to the demands of the religious right. White House objectives were reinforced by the lawyers' emphasis on securing the approval and legitimation of the courts for agency actions.

The political appointees quickly emerged as influential participants. In a high-stakes policy arena such as this, with controversial, salient goals, matters were too important to be left to civil servants, and accountability to elected officials became a key concern. Technical uncertainty reinforced the perceived legitimacy of intervention by "generalists." The political executives consolidated their influence by shifting the nature of the dispute over parental notification. One might have thought that policy discussion within the Office of Adolescent Pregnancy Programs (OAPP) would have centered around cause-effect relationships: for example, would notification decrease contraceptive use or improve parent-child communication? Although many of the public comments and some of the permanent bureaucrats posed precisely these kinds of questions, the dispute evolved instead into one over the duties of government and the values government should pursue. Here, political executives were on firmer ground, able to consider values rather than technologies perhaps better left to "experts." In turn, the decision process moved toward cells 5 and 6. As perceived uncertainty and controversy decreased inside DHHS (technical uncertainty became less relevant, while political appointees moved to define operative goals), hierarchy became a viable governance mechanism. Meanwhile, experts had little basis for seeking representation in the evolving collegial strategy sessions.

At the same time, lawyers were ubiquitous (as they are in rule making generally; West, 1987, pp. 10, 15). The head of the comment analysis team was an attorney; members of the Office of the General Counsel met continuously with her and with the OAPP director. A Department of Justice attorney appeared on the scene long before the comments had been classified. This surfeit of lawyers and their projections of likely court reactions evidently helped move the collegial structure from cell 6 to cell 8. Consideration began to focus on fashioning a case for the final rule. The comments were examined so as to marshal evidence to support the department's position. Note that this shift in focus was another potent means of containing technical uncertainty. It converted questions of cause and effect to the language of rights and duties; the ability to predict outcomes and identify causal processes receded in importance in the face of moral imperatives. Technical controversy rose, but it concerned the legal defensibility of the proposed rule rather than its feasibility or substantive effects (cf. Morse, 1984, p. 66). Meanwhile, controversy over goals disappeared almost by fiat as values became arguments to be bolstered in a legal brief.

This extended example also points to a third factor shaping perceptions of problem settings—the existing governance structures themselves. While the "objective" problem setting remained roughly the same, governance structures evolved and multiplied, in the process altering prevailing perceptions of the decision context. In general, social scientists know relatively little about the effects of structure (Frederickson, 1986), but some potential influences can be identified. As the informal decision structure became more adjudicative in the rule-making case, for instance, it reduced a complex, "polycentric" problem to a two-sided one (Fuller, 1978). Instead of attempting to fashion a reasonable and workable solution, parties took extreme positions; they refused to explore or recognize the legitimacy of value conflicts, and they ignored broad areas of technical uncertainty (cf. Popper, 1983, p. 258). Many argue that these results are hard-wired into adjudicative structures (e.g., Horowitz, 1977; Melnick, 1983). Similarly, democratic theorist Jane Mansbridge contends that whether parties choose adversarial or consensual forms of decision making will shape as well as mirror their perceptions of the extent to which they share interests (1980, pp. 174, 261, 295–96).

Several of these variables—interpretations of legitimacy, organizational permeability, the distribution and dynamics of power, prevailing governance structures—both mold and reflect organizational ideologies. Ideology, in turn, may set important limits on the range of structures deemed relevant and appropriate by members of the organization. As a result, hierarchy occupies a privileged place in U.S. government organizations. Meanwhile, in DHHS, the lawyers' "culture" placed little value on exploring the diverse values and technical ambiguities involved in the parental notification rule, as a more appropriate collegial-competitive structure might have encouraged. The lawyers concentrated instead on preparing a legal defense of the proposed rule.

WHY HIERARCHY?

Thus, numerous factors help explain why actual governance structures will not always be those recommended in table 3. Still, a significant anomaly deserves more focused attention. Chapter 4 asserted that government organizations often act in policy arenas that cannot be characterized by goal consensus and technical certainty—the setting for which hierarchy is best suited. Yet we have also proposed, and casual observation suggests, that hierarchical structures dominate public agencies (cf. Perrow, 1984, pp. 334–35).[3] We now explore three broad explanations for this apparent clustering of structures in cell 5.

Responses to Uncertainty and Controversy

First is the familiar but powerful argument that organizations and decision makers strive to reduce their *perceived* uncertainty or controversy (e.g., Crozier, 1964; Cyert & March, 1963; March & Simon, 1958; J. Thompson, 1967). This argument suggests that organizations will strain to move toward the center of table 3. Even when uncertainty or controversy seems to an observer to be fundamental and, at least in the short run, irreducible, organizational actors will seek to redefine the situation in a way that minimizes or diverts attention from ambiguities or tensions (cf. M. Meyer, 1979, p. 30; Warwick, 1975, p. 85). For example, organizations may rely on experts to absorb uncertainty, "analycitizing politics" to avoid goal ambiguity (S. Taylor, 1984, p. 321), or using selectively gathered technical information to legitimize decisions (Sabatier, 1978, p. 396). Public organizations may adopt management techniques like planning-programming-and-budgeting systems (PPBS) or design elaborate management information systems (see, e.g., Balutis, 1986) as part of an effort to convince watchful legislators and critical citizens that organizational problems are under control (cf. DiMaggio & Powell, 1983, p. 152).

Nor is emphasizing technique the only strategy available. We saw earlier that political appointees shifted discussion about the parental notification rule from the controversy surrounding its potential effects to the moral duties of government. Here, the rule's advocates were on stronger ground, able to argue for the primacy of such a policy goal and against the relevance of the technical dispute (cf. Lange, 1988). This shift also made hierarchy a more viable way of structuring decision making.

These dynamics are reinforced by the fact that actors within organizations strive to manipulate uncertainty (Crozier, 1964; Pfeffer & Salancik, 1978). While it may be in an actor's interest to increase perceived uncertainty for others in order to gain influence, those who are influential must act as though uncertainty is minimal. In 1981, for example, David Stockman, director of the Office of Management and Budget (OMB), held the budget axe over the heads of agency officials and capitalized on his ability to set the economic assumptions that drove deficit estimates. Yet his decisions on budget requests reflected considerably greater confidence about economic relationships and the priorities of the Reagan administration than even Stockman could ultimately muster (Stockman, 1986).

In addition, we have noted the ways in which existing structures shape perceptions of decision contexts. Hierarchical authority can define values

---

3 The dominance of hierarchy also seems to obtain in "professional" organizations (Benveniste, 1987, p. 94); DiMaggio and Powell (1983) assert that it holds in both the public and private sectors.

and procedures so that problem settings either are forced to fit or are treated as "irrelevant" or "insoluble." Significantly, such structuring is a potent means of containing uncertainty and conflict. It can translate questions of cause and effect into the language of hierarchical prerogative and obligation; the ability to predict outcomes and identify causal processes may recede in importance in the face of appeals to such values as respect for precedent.

Finally, *interorganizational* dynamics may be involved. DiMaggio and Powell contend that, as goals become more ambiguous or controversial and technical uncertainty rises, organizations increasingly model themselves after other organizations (1983, pp. 154–55). In such cases, organizations may be heavily dependent upon appearances for legitimacy. Hence, they "may find it to their advantage to meet the expectations of important constituencies about how they should be designed and run" (DiMaggio & Powell, 1983, p. 155; cf. M. Meyer, 1979; J. Thompson, 1967). Meeting these expectations also allows organizations to avoid disruptive internal efforts to reconcile goals or select among technologies. Given the prevalence of hierarchical structures and the general legitimacy accorded to them, most of the structural change within organizations likely is in the direction of increased hierarchy (DiMaggio & Powell, 1983, pp. 147–48).

When scholars view organizations as control systems, they can do little to counterbalance this emphasis on reducing uncertainty and minimizing controversy. They concentrate instead on achieving technical control, stressing the need for and the possibility of finding ways to *solve* discrete "problems."

This is not to say that political scientists have neglected the impact of uncertainty and controversy. Indeed, it is a commonplace in policy studies to point out fundamental ambiguities. Implementation analyses, for example, emphasize complex policy processes and sometimes ask whether it is possible to link organizational actions and outcomes. Often noted, too, are the barriers introduced by disputes among key actors. Yet many of these examinations *end* by observing that chances for "effective implementation" increase as goal consensus and technical certainty increase—the very conditions that they contend only rarely obtain (cf. Browne & Wildavsky, 1984; Stout, 1980). Thus, analyses come full circle: scholars explain shortcomings in implementation by relying on more or less explicit "political" models, yet offer prescriptions that flow from an understanding of organizations as control systems.

Government Agencies as Dependent Systems

One of the reasons for the pervasiveness of hierarchy, then, may be the strain of organization theorists and practitioners alike toward decreasing uncertainty and minimizing controversy; hierarchy appears well adapted to settings with high or increasing goal consensus and technical certainty.

This tendency may be even stronger in *public* organizations for a second reason: the reluctance of citizens, politicians, agency officials, and scholars to think about government agencies as even partially autonomous systems—that is, as entities that should contribute independently to the formulation and implementation of policy (cf. Kaufman, 1981, p. 192; Mashaw, 1983). In the United States, organizations in the executive branch are subject to the demands and oversight of diverse external actors: among them, constituents, clients, members of Congress, congressional subcommittees, the Office of Management and Budget, the president and White House staff, the courts, and state and local governments. Empirically, each of these may press for agency responsiveness to the outsider's interests. Collectively, they provide the rationale for the belief that an agency should be directly accountable to those outside, adding little of its own expertise, insight, or sense of direction to policy making.

This belief places a high premium on the openness or permeability of government organizations to external actors, although the issue of who ought to be influential in what kinds of ways sparks continuing debate. Meanwhile, the demand that public agencies be directed from the outside suggests that they should not be entrusted with much discretion when confronting uncertainty or controversy. Following Woodrow Wilson (1887), "politics" and "administration" are seen as elements that *should* be separated, with the pertinent tasks assigned to different institutions (cf. R. Denhardt, 1984, p. 181).

The dichotomy between "politics" (or "policy") and "administration" shapes most actors' perspectives of executive branch agencies. Legislators, for example, "prefer not to derogate their importance by advertising that it is [less] than it appears to be, and when they do it is usually to denounce administrative . . . 'usurpation' of legislative powers" (Mosher, 1968, p. 6). Terry Moe reports similar dynamics in the White House: prescriptions for presidential leadership "become, through translation, the requirements of good management. Fundamentally political problems emerge with fundamentally non-political solutions" (1985, p. 266).

Agency ideologies push in the same direction, albeit for sometimes different reasons. Warwick argues that, according to the pervasive "managerial philosophy" in the federal executive branch, "efficiency requires a clean line of authority from top to bottom in the organization" (1975, p. 69). Moreover, many agency officials—perhaps especially professionals—see themselves as having little influence on "policy" and as engaging instead in "technical" work to implement political mandates (see, e.g., Gruber, 1987; Mosher, 1968; Rourke, 1984, p. 206). Whether these individuals recognize it or not, of course, their claims to "neutral competence" may enhance their influence over politics and policy by obscuring it: "[T]o the degree that top-level bureaucrats do have autonomous political influence, it is generally because they are able to use the cloak of neutrality, the aura of professional expertise, and the hierarchical control of their organizations as political resources" (Knott & Miller, 1987, p. 194; cf. Lewis, 1980).

For our immediate purposes, the actual extent of "undercover influence" is not important. Whether agency officials genuinely believe that they should engage only in "administration," or whether they merely hide behind the distinction between politics and administration, the dichotomy appears to be a fundamental component of prevailing organizational ideologies.

That the politics-administration dichotomy so dominates our thinking makes hierarchy a compelling structural response to policy problems. Hierarchy provides elected officials with at least the appearance of top-down control, promoting "overhead democracy." Especially as the perceived performance of government agencies falls and citizens and their elected representatives demand "results," pressures for external control through strong reporting and monitoring requirements may be expected to mount (see, e.g., Chubb, 1988; Romzek & Dubnick, 1987). As Seidman and Gilmour observe, "Flawed and imperfect as they may be, the orthodox 'principles' [of administration] remain the only simple, readily understood, and comprehensive set of guidelines available to President and Congress for resolving problems of executive branch structure" (1986, p. 9). Anticipating such a reaction may lead agencies to choose decision structures based on their legitimacy rather than their potential for improving performance (DiMaggio & Powell, 1983, pp. 148–150; M. Meyer, 1979, pp. 199–203).

At the same time, hierarchy may appeal to those inside government organizations. For individuals, it "allows . . . easier access to some status and imparts a feeling of control or influence over their organizational life" (Kraus, 1980, p. 70; cf. Warwick, 1975). Hierarchy also brings organizational benefits. It permits agencies to appear to key external constituencies to be in control (Stout, 1980, p. 29). Especially as hierarchy becomes embedded in civil service rules and traditions, it helps protect agency officials from the vagaries of public opinion and from congressional and presidential "interference" (cf. Benveniste, 1987, p. 267). Indeed, for many officials, hierarchy "is the *only* operating model of organizations to which they have been exposed, one with which they have lived" (Warwick, 1975, p. 71, his emphasis).

Of course, hierarchy never operates perfectly, and considerable leakage of authority and power can be expected (Downs, 1967). Auxiliary checks (congressional oversight, investigations by the General Accounting Office, citizen advisory committees, rule-making procedures, judicial review) develop to plug or at least channel the seepage.

All this implies an understanding of public bureaucracies as dependent entities that is misleading because it is incomplete. By not treating government bureaucracies as at least partially autonomous, observers tend to overlook the reasons such agencies were created in the first place: to pursue strategies beyond the time perspective of most elected officials, to serve as repositories for social learning, and to bring technical, political, and organizational expertise to bear on complex policy problems. This latter view of public organizations promotes what we have called bureaucratic rationality; it also makes agency officials themselves "representatives" of a certain cluster of values and interests (cf. Wood, 1988).

Too often, too, enhancing agency accountability is taken to mean turning to hierarchy. As we saw in chapter 5, however, accountability requires only that decision makers be identifiable and able to be held responsible for their actions. Public administrators have long argued over whether such responsibility must be enforced by those outside the organization (e.g., Finer, 1941; cf. Riley, 1987) or whether internal norms and values can promote agency accountability (e.g., Friedrich, 1940; cf. Burke, 1986; Rourke, 1984). One need not stake out a definite position in the debate to observe that accountability may flow from a variety of mechanisms, not just from hierarchical structures. For example, advocates of mediation contend that codes of ethics—enforced within agencies and by courts—can keep mediated decisions within the bounds prescribed by law and by elected officials (see, e.g., Bacow & Wheeler, 1984, ch. 10; Susskind, 1981). "Participation rights" in an agency's decision making often may be accorded to those outside, ranging from legislative staff to private sector experts to citizen representatives. Even in very complex, technical decision making (such as risk assessment for toxic materials), citizens might be included by being allowed to "exercise peremptory challenges to scientists selected by government administrators as peer reviewers" (J. Lawler & Parle, 1988, p. 15). These sorts of innovations likely would increase representativeness as well as accountability. Of course, they might also reduce bureaucratic rationality. Still, the larger point remains: agency accountability can be enhanced in a number of ways. Not all of them will be appropriate in all cases; as with governance structures more generally, a range of mechanisms probably is needed.

Seeing public agencies only as dependent bodies to be controlled from the outside through hierarchical mechanisms likely undercuts efforts to improve governmental performance through restructuring. On the one hand, our earlier analysis indicates that insistence on hierarchy may leave agencies ill-prepared to operate in policy arenas characterized by a high degree of goal or technical uncertainty or conflict. On the other hand, the demand for responsiveness to outsiders may further increase internal uncertainty and controversy as agencies are opened up at many levels to disputes over values and appropriate policy technologies. Thus, public organizations are buffeted by expectations that push them toward cell 5 and pull them back into cells 1 and 9 while explicitly providing structuring and legitimation only for the former. If reorganization rarely seems to enhance performance, that may not reflect the insignificance of structural change so much as an unnecessary restriction on the range of structural forms and the associated justifications that reformers consider. Reformers are constrained to think about changing arrangements for *control*, but the problems frequently are those of *governance*.

Once more, organizational analysts cannot escape these criticisms unscathed. Because they have failed to view public agencies as partially autonomous, scholars have never developed a "positive model of governmental administration" (Diver, 1981; cf. Stewart, 1975). Practitioners have therefore been left to turn to the private sector for assistance (see, e.g., Balutis, 1986), despite considerable evidence that lessons learned in the world of business either are not directly transferable to government (e.g., Lynn, 1981) or are useful only at the margins, in helping with programmable tasks (e.g., Wholey, Abramson, & Bellavita, 1986).

Control and Governance

The final reason for the prevalence of hierarchy is that, as we saw in chapter 3, few structures have just one function. The hierarchical structures we deem lacking for governance may perform control functions for which they are better suited. A hierarchical structure may respond poorly to uncertainty and controversy in the relevant policy arena but work quite well in coordinating the daily tasks of agency employees and in making it possible for supervisors to guide and assess performance. Organizational "nuts and bolts" activities like reporting and supervision typically are best handled by hierarchies, at least from the vantage point of top managers. And these activities are important, especially to managers who can expect to be evaluated on their performance of such tasks. The inclination to view and evaluate organizations from the control system perspective is thus reinforced by the fact that it often seems plausible and defensible, even where it is fundamentally inadequate.

The Prevalence of Hierarchy

Thus, at least three reasons can be advanced for the prevalence of hierarchy: it enables organizations to minimize their perceived uncertainty and controversy, to fulfill expectations that government agencies be dependent systems, and to handle control as well as governance tasks. The evident result is the "variety attenuation" in organizational responses that Gawthrop (1984, pp. 84ff) so strongly criticizes. For example, organizations react to uncertainty by trying to reduce the ways in which they respond to ambiguous external stimuli. This strategy, in turn, hampers organizations' capacity to anticipate or very quickly detect change in the environment, which intensifies surprise and magnifies consequent uncertainty, triggering another turn of an increasingly vicious circle. The consequence is likely to be poor (or at least incomplete) institutional adaptation to changing environmental demands and expectations, including continued reliance on less appropriate decision structures.

Initially, the implications of our analysis seem bleak. Public organizations seem ill-equipped to respond to the fundamental and irreducible uncertainty and controversy in which they are frequently embedded. Perhaps, given the many constraints on government, organizational redesign is largely futile. Pondering the organization of the White House, Stephen Hess despaired: "Trying to create useful structures becomes an attempt to nail currant jelly to the wall" (1976, p. 177).

We are more hopeful, however. The governance model expands the conceptual repertoire for thinking and speaking about organizational structure, thus encouraging analysts to explore more fully how public organizations do, might, and should make decisions. The model also points to the need for structural experimentation and for "custom-designing" structures to fit problem environments (cf. Gormley, 1986a).

What is most critical, though, is a recognition by analysts and policy makers alike that public organizations *inevitably* confront high levels of uncertainty and controversy. While many decisions can be programmed, policy arenas and problems are apparently becoming more complex and ill-structured. Highly salient "major" issues typically will be plagued with uncertainty or conflict. The key challenge in policy making may well *not* be finding the most efficient or effective means of achieving organizational control or increasing productivity—endeavoring, in effect, to move problems into cell 5. Rather, the challenge will involve learning how to cope with turbulence, controversy, and ambiguity.

CHAPTER SEVEN

Governance Networks

As important as individual governance structures are, in most organizations any one decision may traverse several structures. Moreover, policy
decisions frequently involve players in many government agencies and at
several levels of government, as well as those outside of government
altogether. To get a fuller picture of the dynamics of policy decision making
and of the complexities confronting government organizations, we turn our
attention to the examination of what we call *governance networks,* which
arise from, or are created through, the meshing of governance structures
within and across organizations.

Although we are shifting the level of analysis from structures to networks, the governance model continues to provide an alternative view of
organizational decision making and policy dynamics. In particular, it highlights "constitutional" issues such as the design and evaluation of patterns
of governance within and among organizations.

THE CONCEPT OF GOVERNANCE NETWORKS

Governance structures, especially those deep inside organizations, seldom
stand alone. Instead, they are linked in *networks* through which ideas and
potential decisions pass before final acceptance or rejection.[1] Networks link
the "individuals, groups, and organizations at different levels of govern-

---

1 Networks that extend beyond organizational boundaries are roughly equivalent to
what James D. Thompson (1967) calls organizational "task domains" and Van de Ven and
Ferry (1980) refer to as "interorganizational sets" (see also Tirole, 1986, p. 207). What
Bozeman labels "governance structures" (1987, p. 67ff) are closer to our "governance networks." Sociologists probably have used network analysis most extensively; see, for

ment, and in both public and private sectors, that act together in the formation and implementation of policy in particular policy areas. An agency will be inextricably linked with such a network, and different subunits of large agencies are usually involved in different networks" (Rainey & Milward, 1983, p. 140; cf. Hanf, 1978, p. 12). *Governance* networks link the governance structures these actors rely upon in making decisions. Thus, including them in one's analysis provides a more complete picture of policy making. Both organizations and policy arenas can be understood as encompassing one or more governance networks.

Governance networks link structures both within and across organizational boundaries. Like governance structures, networks may be permanent or temporary, formal or informal. They may be consciously designed, emerge unplanned from the decisions of several actors, or simply evolve. A given governance structure may be part of one or several networks.

Governance networks may bring very different kinds of decision structures to bear upon a particular policy problem. For instance, the framers of the U.S. Constitution constructed a complex network, incorporating separation of powers, checks and balances, and federalism into their plan for national governance. On a much smaller scale, the White House boasts numerous networks, some the products of conscious design, others the results of unplanned evolution. The complicated path of a domestic policy decision early in the Reagan administration illustrates the linking of discrete structures into a planned network: issues flowed from subcabinet-level interagency groups through a cabinet council, the White House Office of the Cabinet Secretary, sometimes the Office of Policy Development, and finally to the senior staff and perhaps the president. In contrast, the decision dynamics revealed during the Iran-contra hearings demonstrate the way in which informal networks may evolve in the absence of explicit direction.

The notion of governance networks is likely to be especially important when studying public organizations. Governmental decisions rarely are simple, one-time choices. Instead, they typically are characterized by long and complex chains of events and numerous reconsiderations. The concept of networks helps to capture these often fragmented policy processes, where decisions involve multiple bureaus and agencies, members of Congress, White House staffers, the courts, interest groups, and other levels of government.

Governance networks are at least implicit in most discussions of policy dynamics. Treatments of policy "subsystems," for instance, recognize the need to look beyond organizational boundaries. The "iron triangles" and "issue networks" so frequently mentioned in the literature on U.S. public policy are prime examples of the networks that link organizations across

example, Galaskiewicz (1979), Laumann (1976), Laumann, Galaskiewicz, & Marsden (1978), and Perrow (1986, pp. 192–208). In political science, Meltsner and Bellavita discuss "policy networks," which encompass not only governance structures but also "the constellation of actors, institutions, [and] issues . . . that make up a policy arena" (1983, p. 44; cf. Sabatier, 1987; Sabatier & Pelkey, 1987).

branches and levels of government and between the public and private sectors. Derisively labeled "unholy alliances" and, more dispassionately, "subgovernments," iron triangles link executive branch bureaucrats, legislative committees and subcommittees, and interest groups. Characterized by close and mutually beneficial ties, these networks often are closed to the public and to chief executives and their appointees. Defense procurement decisions, for example, are allegedly forged by members of Congress interested in bringing government contracts to their districts (and receiving campaign contributions from contractors), lower-level Pentagon officials anxious to remain on good terms with congressional committees and perhaps thinking of eventual private sector jobs, and representatives of the defense industry. This is a caricature at best, especially at a time when irate legislators thunder about "$2,000 coffee pots" and the Defense Department imposes additional controls on contractors. Indeed, it is likely that few actual policy networks are as impregnable as the metaphor of iron triangles suggests (cf. Jordan, 1981, pp. 99ff). Similarly, the weakening of the mighty tobacco subsystem indicates that networks may change significantly over time (e.g., Fritschler, 1983). Even so, as policy arenas come to resemble iron triangles, they are probably better able to reach decision closure (an element of bureaucratic rationality), but at the risk of failing to consider all relevant information (the other requirement for bureaucratic rationality) and of reducing representativeness, accountability, and legitimacy.

At the other end of the spectrum are so-called issue networks, as described by Heclo:

> Participants move in and out of the networks constantly. Rather than groups united in dominance over a program, no one . . . is in control of the policies and issues. Any direct material interest is often secondary to intellectual or emotional commitments. (1978, p. 102)

Thus, a policy arena like that surrounding proposed reforms in the financing of health care may attract numerous participants. The list may seem endless: members of Congress and their staffs; officials of the U.S. Department of Health and Human Services and the Office of Management and Budget; White House policy advisers; groups representing for-profit, not-for-profit, and public hospitals; private insurers; representatives of doctors, other health care providers, and medical educators; state officials concerned with rising Medicaid costs; state, county, and local bureaucrats; and a host of consumer groups, each with its own constituencies (for example, the elderly, children, pregnant adolescents, people with AIDS). Participation by these players is likely to be fluid and intermittent, alignments and coalitions fragile. Although issue networks, unlike iron triangles, may boost inclusiveness (a component of representativeness) and broaden the information available to policy makers (contributing to bureaucratic rationality), they may militate against achieving decision closure and threaten legitimacy (Heclo, 1978, pp. 118–21).

In addition to highlighting decision dynamics involving more than one governance structure, focusing on governance networks helps link the governance model with other approaches to organizations. Examining networks may increase our understanding of the problems of coordination emphasized by those who view organizations as control systems. Interagency committees, for example, may permit officials from departments with overlapping jurisdictions to settle conflicts or work out resource-sharing agreements. At the same time, examining networks may help account for the preoccupation of top agency officials with trying to "gain control" of their organizations, often by imposing more stringent rules and reporting requirements. Heightened control both seems necessary and is likely to be elusive, for public agencies are frequently "cross-cut and fragmented" by demands from numerous network actors (Rainey & Milward, 1983, p. 144).

Likewise, the emergence of networks may at times resemble the evolutionary dynamics expected by natural systems theorists. Through the 1970s, for instance, the environmental policy arena shifted from a closed network, with only a few, "expert" participants, to an open network teeming with actors; this evolution evidently reflected the influence of such external forces as growing public distrust of government and technology, rising concern with the fouling of the physical environment, and mounting demands for citizen participation in policy making (see, e.g., the summary in McCabe & Fitzgerald, 1987).

The concept of governance networks, then, seems to provide a fruitful way of thinking about both policy decision making and the constraints and opportunities facing individual organizations. The current work on networks, however, is not fully satisfactory. Paul Sabatier, for example, criticizes many analyses of iron triangles and issue networks for excluding such key actors as journalists, analysts, and researchers (1987, p. 659). He also points to the need to examine networks embedded in other networks: so-called "advocacy coalitions"—themselves networks—interact as participants in policy subsystems (1987, p. 661). More generally, as helpful as the ideas of iron triangles and issue networks are, most actual networks seem to fall between the polar opposites. Nor are the concepts fully applicable to the linking of governance structures *within* public organizations. Finally, and perhaps most important, few discussions of networks stress their characteristic patterns of decision making. Instead, most analyses use the idea of networks to delineate major actors and describe their relationships.

TYPES OF GOVERNANCE NETWORKS

Table 5 addresses some of the problems just discussed by presenting a classification of governance networks. While the listing is illustrative rather than exhaustive, it should provide a better sense of the notion of governance networks as well as suggest the range of possible types. Each type of network is characterized in terms of its dominant pattern of interaction.

The descriptions in the table represent *analytical* categories; instances of them are rarely seen in pure form, and "hybrid" networks seem quite likely. Our examples, then, are mainly suggestive of what a particular kind of governance network might look like in practice. Recall, too, that networks link governance structures; the structures in any one network may be of varying types. With these cautions in mind, let us examine each type of network.

Bureaucratic

Most familiar are bureaucratic networks, which link structures through standardized reporting procedures and hierarchical authority relationships. Participation rights in these networks (Cohen, March, & Olsen, 1976; Jordan, 1981) are based on position in the mandated hierarchy. Bureaucratic networks tend to be stable; rules and routines become reinforced by habits and norms of participation.

Not surprisingly, bureaucratic networks abound in government. Since the Nixon years, for example, the Office of Management and Budget (OMB) increasingly has become involved in reviewing agency decisions. President Reagan formalized "administrative central clearance" with Executive Order 12498, which requires agencies to notify OMB in writing if they are planning or conducting "significant regulatory actions." This involves OMB in more than mere paper shuffling. As the office has moved more and more into "command mode" (Aberbach & Rockman, 1987, p. 15; cf. Moe, 1985), complaints have mounted about this "bureaucratic KGB that secretly kills, defangs, or alters regulations" (Kriz, 1987, p. 1404; cf. Bryner, 1987, pp. 82–83). As chapter 6 would lead one to expect, bureaucracy is probably a very common governance network, especially inside agencies and within the executive branch, even when its component structures are not themselves hierarchies. Indeed, most government agencies are bureaucratic networks. They usually are more complex than mere bureaucracies, but they are at least that.

Team

In contrast, other networks emphasize collaboration and collegiality. "Teams" both reflect and seek to foster shared values and trust among members of different governance structures. This type of network is close to what Ouchi (1980) calls "clans." Teams work to encourage a sense of group membership and strive toward consensus. The importance of developing trust and good working relationships indicates that teams typically will seek stable membership.

Table 5 Types of Organizational Polities

Network	Characteristics			
	Means of Linkage	Basis of Participation Rights	Level of Stability	Decision Rule
Bureaucratic	Rules, routines	Position	High	SOPs, decision by top authority
Team	Shared values, trust	"Group" members	Moderate to high	Consensus
Decentralized	Competition, mutual adjustment	Open	Low	Indeterminate
Confrontational	Clash of opposing views	Representatives of opposing views	Low to moderate	Decision by uninvolved party
Bargaining	Negotiation among advocates	Representatives of competing positions	Moderate	Voting rule
Consultative	Transmission of expertise	Experts, clients	Variable	Client choice
Appeals	Reconsideration of decision	Parties to decision	Moderate to high	Variable

Taking over an organization beleaguered by the Iran-contra scandal and torn by internal sniping, Reagan Chief of Staff Howard Baker experimented with a team-based network linking senior White House staffers and their subordinates. The organization chart "looks like the Olympic flag . . . [with] five overlapping power centers or clusters" (Kirschten, 1987b [4 April], p. 824). To at least a limited extent, the strategy worked. By late summer, staffers reported: "'There isn't much intrigue anymore . . . [T]hings have become very boring' on the White House infighting front" (Kirschten, 1987b [1 August], p. 1982). As this example suggests, teams are most likely to emerge where the presence or impact of routines is relatively low.

Decentralized

Decentralized networks rely on interaction and competition for linkage (cf. Ouchi, 1980). Participation may be quite fluid, and decisions emerge from the interplay of actors. Decision making in these networks resembles the "garbage can" processes described by organized-anarchy theorists (e.g., Cohen, March, & Olsen, 1976) as well as the mutual adjustment praised by early pluralists (e.g., Lindblom, 1959). To the extent that "coordination" occurs, it grows out of ongoing, informal interaction among participants and depends on the skills and inclinations of individuals in the network.

Competition often may appear in decentralized policy networks, reflecting overlapping jurisdictions, different missions, and scarce resources. For instance, foreign intelligence is gathered and interpreted by the Central Intelligence Agency, the Defense Intelligence Agency, and units in the State Department (Krepon, 1987), all of whose data and analyses can differ dramatically. Similarly, the U.S. Forest Service, Fish and Wildlife Service, National Park Service, Bureau of Land Management, and Bureau of Outdoor Recreation all manage federal land (Sapolsky, 1977).

Confrontational

Like many decentralized networks, confrontational networks include clashing participants. Here, however, opposition is more contained: participation may be restricted at the outset, and an uninvolved party makes the final decision. Confrontational networks, while less fluid than decentralized networks, may be only moderately stable, since decision makers likely will seek to quasi-resolve conflict (Cyert & March, 1963), only intermittently relying on the network.

Presidents routinely referee violent disagreements among representatives of conflicting structures, as do department heads and Congress. The Nuclear Waste Policy Act of 1982 mandates a more formal confrontational network for siting nuclear waste disposal operations. It pits the U.S. Department of Energy, with responsibility for screening and selecting sites, against potential host states. The latter can halt development of a site by notifying Congress of their disapproval. Congress, however, holds the ultimate authority: state refusal can be overridden by a majority vote of both houses (Downey, 1985).

Bargaining

In bargaining networks, participants again take differing positions, but decisions reflect compromise and negotiation among the advocates themselves. To facilitate bargaining, participation rights are limited to representatives of opposing positions, and efforts typically will be made to keep participation stable. Since consensus on a negotiated outcome may be difficult to achieve, participants also are likely to develop rules for reaching closure, such as majority vote or provision for vetoes.

The federal regional councils established by Richard Nixon in 1972 evidently provided forums for bargaining among officials of federal agencies in Washington and in the field, staff of different domestic departments, state and local officials, and technical experts from the public and private sectors. Although President Reagan disbanded the councils in 1983, they are credited with, for example, helping fashion the Negotiated Investment Strategy approach used in Columbus, Ohio, Gary, Indiana, and St. Paul, Minnesota, to promote intergovernmental cooperation in developing initiatives aimed at urban revitalization (Gage, 1984).

Similarly, administrative regulations often emerge from a process of bargaining among groups in and out of government. The late 1960s and 1970s saw considerable expansion in the number and variety of parties involved, including consumer advocates and environmentalists. Within the executive branch, President Carter's Regulatory Council brought together the heads of major regulatory agencies and commissions to resolve interagency disputes and negotiate coordination (Bryner, 1987, p. 71).

Consultative

Consultative networks put less stress on the expression of opposing views than on the transmission of expertise between experts and their clients, the actual decision makers (e.g., Eulau, 1986, pp. 496–500; note, too, the similarity to Benveniste's "senior staff model," 1987, pp. 88–90). Clients may rely on the same or a changing array of experts, choosing whose advice to follow and whose to ignore.

Top-level government officials frequently turn to this sort of network and may feature it as a central element of their strategies for governing. Throughout his presidency, Herbert Hoover consulted with numerous economists, industrialists, and labor leaders. His evident failures were in ignoring or downplaying information that challenged his favored strategies and in refusing to expand the circle of experts with whom he consulted (Walcott & Hult, forthcoming; cf. W. Barber, 1975).

Some efforts have been made to institutionalize consultation in the policy process. For example, in 1980 the Environmental Protection Agency established the Health Effects Institute to generate and evaluate health data on auto emissions for use within EPA and by other policy makers. The Institute's Board of Directors appoints two scientific boards—for Health Research and Health Review—to establish policy, oversee results, and publish scientific data (Morse, 1984, pp. 104–5). Morse (1984) argues that Congress should establish an Environmental Consultation Service to "review environmental regulations so that the views of diverse environmental stakeholders are considered in detail before regulations are adopted" (p. 121). It is always difficult, of course, to ensure that decision makers consider such advice. Clearly, more useful consultative networks will link structures that elicit a range of relevant inputs, with policy makers actively seeking information. Participation in such a network can be indispensable for an administrator or an agency seeking to play an effective policy role (cf. Heclo, 1977).

Appeals

Once made, decisions may be reconsidered by a separate body. In some cases, appeal may be automatic, as in the denial of eligibility for certain assistance programs; in other cases, parties with legal or political "standing" may urge review. Grounds for overturning decisions may vary from neglect of particular substantive criteria to failure to follow certain procedural requirements.

Most structures and networks in U.S. governments are embedded in an appeals network, since government actions (and inaction) are subject to judicial review. Appeals need not be restricted to the courtroom, however. Cabinet officials and bureau chiefs sometimes challenge OMB budget decisions by taking their cases to the White House staff or even to the president. In the Nixon and Ford administrations, OMB coordinated a "'quality of life review' . . . which allowed agencies opposed to [decisions of the Environmental Protection Agency] to get a second hearing" (Waterman, 1987, p. 7). At these reviews, OMB officials examined the economic impact and feasibility of EPA actions, going beyond EPA's concern with protecting public health and the physical environment. Similarly, in President Reagan's first term, the Cabinet Council on Natural Resources and the Environment (chaired by Interior Secretary James Watt) oversaw EPA's policy decisions (Waterman, 1987, p. 17), while the Vice President's Task Force on Regulatory Relief reviewed disputes between OMB and the Occupational Safety and Health Administration (Bryner, 1987, p. 132).

APPROPRIATE GOVERNANCE NETWORKS

Conceptually, at least, diverse types of governance networks can be identified. It is more difficult to suggest which networks are appropriate under what circumstances. Shifting from structures to networks introduces manifold complexities. Is each of the structures in the network appropriate for its particular problem environment? Is the network well designed for the decision settings in which it operates? Are the structures appropriate for the network? Moreover, as should be clear from our examples, structures are apt to be embedded in multiple networks, and networks themselves may be intertwined (cf. Eulau, 1986, p. 497). This growing complexity makes it harder to untangle the dynamics of decision making and to apply evaluative standards (cf. Powell, 1985, p. 201).

TABLE 6 Decision Settings and Appropriate Governance Networks

Technical	Goal		
	Uncertainty	**Consensus**	**Controversy**
Uncertainty	1 Decentralized	2 Team	3 Confrontational Bargaining
Certainty	4 Team	5 Bureaucratic	6 Confrontational Bargaining
Controversy	7 Consultative Confrontational	8 Consultative Confrontational Appeals	9 Indeterminate

Still, hints of matches and mismatches between prevailing networks and decision settings can be found in the policy literature. Moreover, as should already be apparent, there are several parallels between the types of governance networks we have outlined and the governance structures described in chapter 3, providing further suggestions for possible prescriptions. Hierarchy and bureaucracy clearly are related, for example, as are adversarial structures and confrontational networks and collegial-competitive structures and bargaining networks. There are also similarities between teams and collegial-consensual structures, decentralized networks and market structures, and appeals networks and adjudicative structures.

Table 6 summarizes our tentative conclusions about appropriate governance networks for particular decision settings. In the following sections we briefly examine each of the cells in the table.

Cell 1: Decentralized Networks

When both goal and technical uncertainty are high, it seems appropriate to allow decisions to emerge from the unguided interplay of key actors. Calls for "redundancy" point to the benefits of overlapping jurisdictions (e.g., Bendor, 1985; Landau, 1969). Harvey Sapolsky (1977), for instance, advocates interjecting competition into the U.S. health care system. Given multiple, difficult-to-prioritize policy goals (emphasizing, for example, provision of primary, chronic, in-hospital acute, and preventive care), three or four independent agencies, each pursuing distinctive missions, should compete to manage federal health programs. This "competition of rival medical hierarchies," each with its own constituencies, might better advance all the goals. A study of six Pacific coast seaports lends some support to this conviction, suggesting that competing public agencies promote more innovation than hierarchically consolidated port authorities (Boschken & Shumaker, 1987).

Still, decentralized networks may have significant disadvantages. For example, they sometimes work against decision closure. The differing estimates of the Soviet military threat produced by competing agencies have made it difficult for top decision makers to take authoritative action in weapons talks (Krepon, 1987). Thus, decentralized networks evidently are more appropriate when uncertainty is high and less useful as controversy rises and becomes polarizing.

Cells 2 and 4: Team Networks

When goals or technologies are uncertain, teams permit exploration for alternatives and probing for possible consequences of particular decision options. Representativeness is likely to be important in choosing team members. When technology is uncertain (cell 2), representation of experts is indicated; when goals are uncertain (cell 4), elected officials, political appointees, citizens, and representatives of stakeholder groups will have greater claims to participation rights.

Teams may be especially useful during the early stages of problem definition. The first task forces to consider the emerging AIDS problem may have resembled teams in bringing together officials from across levels and branches of government and experts from the private sector. As such groups reach consensus or as participants begin to advocate opposing positions, other network types become more appropriate. This may be one reason why teams are particularly likely to be *ad hoc* and temporary, disbanding after a problem is defined or becomes less visible.

Cells 3 and 6: Confrontational and Bargaining Networks

Where goals are controversial, confrontational networks give final decision makers (for instance, the president, agency heads) the opportunity to hear the conflicting sides and to make value choices. Tasks that might benefit from such networks include managing coastlines, regulating pollution, and handling toxic wastes (Downey, 1985, p. 88). Among potential problems are finding legitimate actors to make the final decision (Downey, 1985, p. 92) and ensuring that interested parties will participate and accept the decision as authoritative (Sigmon, 1987).

When there is no acceptable decision maker, or when legitimate decision makers themselves disagree or seek to avoid conflict, bargaining among disputants may become more useful. Presidents such as Eisenhower, Nixon, and Reagan often preferred that others in the executive branch settle differences among themselves, coming to the president only when a final settlement was reached. California is moving toward having local governments, industries, environmental groups, and residents develop their own plans for managing hazardous waste and materials. These bargaining networks would not stand alone, but would be part of a larger network in which the state serves as an arbiter (forming a confrontational network) or appeals board (Mazmanian, 1987).

Cell 5: Bureaucratic Networks

Like hierarchies, bureaucratic networks seem most appropriate in situations characterized by goal consensus and technical certainty. Procedures for awarding grants, for example, often can be spelled out in detail. Local governments may seek the grants, following rules for eligibility and for the form and content of the application. State or federal officials can then evaluate applications using set criteria for such things as need, ability to provide matching funds, and suitability of the proposed project. Funding can be granted or withheld; expenditures can be monitored. Not all programs function so smoothly, of course, but when the goals are clear and agreed upon and the technologies for making the grants certain, bureaucratic networks—with their attendant rules, deadlines, and hierarchical decision authority—appear to be appropriate.

Bureaucracy will be less appropriate in other cases, however. For example, Romzek and Dubnick (1987) fear that NASA's growing reliance on rules and routines heightens the prospects for further disasters like *Challenger* by minimizing the experience and expertise in decisions that can never be fully programmed, given the highly interactive technologies involved (1987, pp. 234–36). More appropriate might be confrontational networks, or teams including contractors, technical experts, quality assurance and safety staffers, and top decision makers, who could better wrestle with the fundamental uncertainties and risks of human space flight.

Cell 7: Consultative and Confrontational Networks

When goals are uncertain and technologies controversial, consultative networks may be called for. Consultation "facilitates the utilization of diverse knowledge and intelligence" (Eulau, 1986, p. 499) but keeps the final decision in the hands of authoritative policy makers who can legitimately articulate goals (cf. Benveniste, 1987, pp. 88–90). Yellin, for example, recommends that regulatory decision makers consult with planning groups in at least two fields, economics and biology:

> [T]he economic planners will attempt to minimize the quantifiable costs of proposed regulations through the use of price incentives. In contrast, the biological planners will tend to emphasize extrapolation to man from the results of *in vitro* toxicity experiments, animal models, or known effects of chemicals and radiation in simple organisms, and exhibit a countervailing preference for health-based standards and direct regulation . . . [T]he two planning groups would report independently on identical policy questions formulated by the agency head. Agencies could then regulate in light of two alternative sets of findings. (Yellin, 1983, pp. 1328–29)

Such consultation should increase the bureaucratic rationality of the final decision by exposing policy makers to a range of information.

Consultative networks also may enhance the legitimacy of the decision by encouraging discussion with those it will affect, thus increasing the likelihood of compliance. Leonard Cole (1987) contends, for example, that the New Jersey Department of Environmental Protection made a serious mistake in its efforts to respond to the controversy over alleged radon contamination of homes by not seeking the advice of local officials; the department instead tried to exercise top-down control, in effect relying on a bureaucratic network to communicate with residents and city officials. The results were unresolved controversy over how to dispose of soil removed from around the afflicted homes, persistent ill will and sniping between state and local officials, and continual delays.

Under such circumstances, consultation readily shades into confrontation. As controversy grows, decision makers may find themselves enmeshed in a network of experts advocating inconsistent technologies. Because goals are uncertain, final decision authority should remain in the hands of elected officials or their agents. Yet, as technical conflict mounts, direct confrontation among experts may generate less consultation and more information about policy options and consequences. In both confrontational and consultative networks, decision makers select those who provide data and analysis; in the former, however, controversies among advisers are more likely to set the scope and content of the policy debate.

Cell 8: Consultative, Confrontational, and Appeals Networks

When goals are agreed upon but there are technical disputes, consultative and confrontational networks can expose policy makers to many points of view and permit them to choose among the competing options, just as in cell 7. Although ubiquitous, appeals networks may be particularly appropriate in such situations. They provide a means of reexamining decisions to ensure that the technical option selected is consistent with prevailing values and goals. Resort to an appeals network may help enhance bureaucratic rationality and accountability, and, hence the legitimacy of policy making. Thus, Yellin advocates incorporating "second opinions" into environmental decision making, with independent review bodies exercising procedural and substantive oversight over decisions (1981, p. 497).

Cell 9: Indeterminate

When goal and technical controversy are both present, no single network type seems most appropriate. What will likely be seen as especially legitimate, however, are linked confrontational and appeals networks. The former provides for the clash of divergent views that is so much a part of the U.S. system of checks and balances and competing interests. An accompanying series of appeals mechanisms may help keep the conflict within bounds while permitting losers other opportunities to influence policy.

Hybrid Networks

Thus far, our discussion has assumed that networks will regularly process decisions having the same characteristics. But clearly this need not be the case. Stable networks—those including roughly the same participants and governance structures—may arise to deal with decisions in a given area, regardless of the uncertainty or controversy surrounding any particular issue. The White House Press Office, for instance, is embedded in a network that links various elements of the administration to the journalistic community. It must handle everything from routine informational requests to probing questions about national goals and possible policy technologies to allegations of impropriety. Some of these inputs will trigger responses that most resemble those of consultative networks, some will lead to the search and transmission procedures characteristic of bureaucratic networks, and some may spark confrontation. Within this network the capacity exists to draw upon an array of governance alternatives; which alternative emerges depends on the problem at hand.

Such hybrid networks may evolve over time, as interdependent institutions develop diverse responses appropriate to the array of issues they must face. Hybrid networks also may be the product of conscious design. The checks and balances built into the U.S. constitutional system, for example, reflect the framers' intent to construct a complex governance network capable of most of the ideal types of network responses we have identified. In general, the higher the "level" of a network—in the example of checks and balances, the governmental system as a whole—the greater the diversity of the choices it will confront, and the more likely and more appropriate will be some form of hybrid network.

In addition, as we have noted, most governance structures in public organizations and in the executive branch as a whole are embedded in bureaucratic networks, with final authority residing in the office of a top executive (departmental secretary, agency director, president, governor). Often, for reason of law or external accountability, decisions made through nonhierarchical structures and nonbureaucratic networks must be accepted and propounded by that top executive. These kinds of routines amount to a hybrid network, inasmuch as they combine hierarchical control with dynamics typically not found in a pure bureaucratic network.

The complexity of policy subsystems and their component networks makes the selection of appropriate networks for particular decision settings a daunting task. To complicate matters further, networks are likely to be very difficult to reshape, since change may send shock waves through their governance structures and other networks.

Despite these difficulties, governance networks are worthy of attention. Moving to higher levels of analysis is important, for governance structures rarely operate in isolation. Moreover, as such structures multiply, they raise additional governance issues, which may trigger the development of still more structures. The new structures generated by and driving this dynamic of governance differentiation (see chapter 3) in turn may change the nature and effects of prevailing networks.

Efforts to respond to particular policy problems often lead to the introduction of governance structures, with consequences for networks. For example, Lyndon Johnson created the Office of Economic Opportunity (OEO) to mobilize governmental resources for his War on Poverty. The Reagan White House responded to the criticisms of the Tower Board by installing "trip wires": covert action findings and other classified national security documents were to be reviewed both by the National Security Adviser and his legal adviser and by Chief of Staff Howard Baker and the White House Counsel's office before they reached the president (Kirschten, 1987b [23 May], p. 1336). As much attention as these particular changes received, their impact on larger networks deserves fuller consideration. For example, only in retrospect could one see the disruptive consequences of OEO for the complex mesh of relationships both within the executive branch and between the federal government and local officials (see also, Landau, 1988).

Thus, focusing on governance networks permits us to examine politics throughout the policy process. This focus underscores the pervasiveness of politics and the challenge of organizational design and governance. Our examination of various governance networks is meant not as an exercise in taxonomy, but rather as a stimulant to thought about possible arrangements for governance and their effects. Again, the challenge of formulating useful organization policy surfaces. For the analysis points, too, to the difficulties of such efforts to change existing patterns of governance: habits, expectations, and legitimizing norms have grown up around them, and alternative arrangements, like present ones, involve troubling value tradeoffs.

These tradeoffs become even more difficult when one focuses on organizations as self-contained (though hardly autonomous) political systems, with implications not only for policy making but also for their members. It is to these issues that we turn next.

CHAPTER EIGHT

Organizational Polities and Citizenship in Organizations

Our analysis began with the notion that organizations can be thought of as polities. Political philosophers have long proposed and evaluated alternative political systems. Plato, for example, sought the "ideal" political system, while Alexis de Tocqueville offered a mixed review of "democracy." More recently, Robert Paul Wolff (1970) has written "in defense of anarchism," and Robert Dahl (1971) has explored the determinants and consequences of a version of representative democracy he calls "polyarchy."

As polities, organizations develop distinctive patterns of governance and the ideologies that support and justify those arrangements. Our examination of diverse organizational polities will highlight "constitutional" issues revolving around the design and assessment of the entire system of governance in organizations.

Perhaps even more important, thinking about organizations as polities inexorably takes us back to the individual, for it raises the issue of "citizenship" in organizations. Most discussions of national political systems pay considerable attention to individuals, whose welfare is the putative end of liberal-democratic polities. Contemporary organization and public administration theorists scarcely have ignored organizational members; scholars have written a great deal about the benefits and costs of various techniques for dealing with employees. Yet an understanding of organizations as control systems pervades most of this work (though see, e.g., Ferguson, 1984; Marini, 1971), and concern typically revolves around the implications of management strategies for enhancing organizational productivity or securing compliance from employees (cf. Perrow, 1986, ch. 3). In contrast, considering organizational members as *citizens* underscores the importance of examining employees' rights as well as their obligations. This viewpoint focuses not only on the impact of individuals on organizations but also on the effects of organizational membership on individuals.

The conceptions of organizations as polities and organizational members as citizens thus go hand in hand. We begin our consideration of these ideas by exploring various possible configurations of politics in organizations and then move to a discussion of the opportunities and limitations they pose for their citizens.

ORGANIZATIONAL POLITICAL SYSTEMS

Focusing on political systems in organizations means shifting levels of analysis once again, this time moving to the organization as a whole. Organizational political systems typically will be made up of intertwined governance networks and structures. In addition, both structures and networks may transcend the boundaries of any one organization, thus linking very different political systems.

Efforts to classify organizational polities are scattered throughout the organization theory literature. Some typologies emphasize the distribution of power in organizations. Khandwalla, for instance, notes that organizations may be "closed, highly centralized hegemonies, competing oligarchies, inclusive hegemonies, or polyarchies" (1977, p. 63). Similarly, Gareth Morgan delineates several "modes of political rule" in organizations, among them autocracy, technocracy, codetermination, and representative democracy (1986, p. 145); Mintzberg lists six "power configurations" (1983, pp. 307ff).

Other discussions stress variations in the ways organizations use their power. Perhaps best known is Amitai Etzioni's (1975) examination of the links between organizational goals and mechanisms for gaining compliance with them. In this view, organizations whose primary aim is to preserve internal order (prisons and mental hospitals, for example) will be "coercive" as they pursue that objective. Those with largely economic goals will rely on "utilitarian" means of attaining compliance (such as wages and "perks"), while organizations with "cultural" objectives (for example, schools and churches) will appeal to the "normative commitments" of their members.

None of these approaches seems fully satisfactory. Most flow from an understanding of organizations as control systems; they emphasize the distribution of power and strategies for aligning employees' values with those of the organization. Correspondingly less attention is given such concerns as the extent and nature of members' participation in organizational decision making and the bases of the political system's legitimacy—staples in analyses of national polities. Moreover, few of these efforts have generated sustained examination of political dynamics within organizations, or of the determinants and consequences of differing political systems.

In this section we build on our earlier examination of governance structures and networks to delineate several possible kinds of organizational polities. We explore, too, some of the factors that might lead to the emergence of particular political systems and the consequences of various system types. Like governance structures and networks, organizational political systems are not always or even typically products of conscious organizational design; rather, they often evolve, more or less undirected, over time.

Our discussion here is brief but, we hope, suggestive. Its purpose is to outline the terms in which a fuller analysis might be carried out and to point to some of the directions such an analysis might take.

Types of Organizational Political Systems

Table 7 profiles five types of organizational polities. The usual caveat applies: actual organizations cannot be neatly pigeonholed into these analytical categories. However, the categories may serve as benchmarks against which existing and proposed organizations can be compared. We believe that most organizations—or at least their major subunits—will come to most resemble one of these types.

Command. We start with a familiar description of government entities: "command" organizations. Dominated by bureaucratic and appeals networks, this type of organizational political system emphasizes hierarchical structures, rule-governed activity, and centralized power. Subunits are "tightly coupled," joined by standardized flows of information and authority. The principal sources of legitimacy for decision making in such an organization are bureaucratic rationality and external accountability. Thus, the image of command organizations has long appealed to reformers (Salamon, 1981) hoping to increase the effectiveness of government organizations as well as their accountability to elected officials. Douglas Morgan's (1987) "Type A" organizations, for example, seek to curb "administrative abuse" and heighten agency accountability by relying on typical features of command systems, such as performance and program audits and formalized rule-making procedures.

Collectivist. "Collectivist" organizations (e.g., Newman, 1980; Rothschild & Whitt, 1986; Rothschild-Whitt, 1979), in contrast, are more collegial. Authority tends to be distributed more equally, and decisions reflect consensus rather than the application of routines or the mandate of a superordinate. Such systems are found with some frequency in educational institutions. Chubb, for example, contrasts command-oriented schools with those characterized by democratic decision making, in which teachers

TABLE 7 Types of Organizational Polities

Polity	Characteristics				
	Internal Coupling	Dominant Network Type	Distribution of Authority	Basis of Participation	Primary Sources of Legitimacy
Command	Tight	Bureaucratic Appeals	Centralized	Position	Bureaucratic rationality Accountability
Collectivist	Tight	Team	Egalitarian	Membership, or designation as representative	Equality Representativeness
Pluralist	Moderate	Bargaining Decentralized Confrontational	Indeterminate	Competing interests	Representativeness
Corporatist	Moderate to tight	Bargaining Consultative	Moderately dispersed	Subunits	Representativeness
Confederated	Loose	Bargaining, with veto	Decentralized	Partially autonomous units	Representativeness Accountability to units

are more involved and influential in establishing disciplinary codes, selecting textbooks, designing curricula, and choosing colleagues (1988, p. 34).

The sense of collective enterprise may be fostered by the organization's leader. One of the marks of the "public entrepreneurs" Eugene Lewis (1980) describes is their ability to create commitment and solidarity among their followers. Still, legitimacy in a collectivist organization is grounded in the organization's ability to maintain some degree of equality and a sense of shared participation in decision making. Many local nonprofit organizations, such as some of those offering services to battered women or drug abusers, at least begin with collectivist norms, using participation and strong common values to help compensate for low pay and draining work (for examples, see those described in Mansbridge, 1980). Douglas Morgan (1987) argues that the development of strong, shared norms limiting administrative discretion actually can enhance agency accountabilty.

Pluralist. "Pluralist" organizations operate through the interplay of representatives of competing interests—for example, when economists, biologists, and lawyers all participate in formulating environmental regulations. As in national political systems, influence in such organizations may be highly concentrated or more diffuse. Legitimacy, though, is likely to flow from the extent of representativeness, which, as we have observed, entails both the inclusion of interested parties and the perception of potential responsiveness to their concerns. Still, William Scott warns that legitimacy may be hard to come by in the absence of a "traditional" or accepted ideology of pluralism within organizations (1969, p. 49).

Corporatist. Another form familiar to students of national polities is the "corporatist" organization. Less fluid than pluralist political systems, corporatist organizations develop more stable, less conflictual modes of group-based decision making. Their dominant network types emphasize bargaining and consultation. Representation remains important, although here it is more fixed, varying less from decision to decision, than in pluralist systems. Participation rules specify more precisely which interests must be included in what sorts of decisions: for example, members of the general counsel's staff might participate in all efforts at writing regulations, and affirmative action officials in all personnel actions. Such specifications for participation mean that influence will be dispersed, though not necessarily equally diffused, through the organization.

Confederated. Subunits gain more influence in "confederated" polities. Coupling is likely to be looser than in other political forms, and subunits may be able to veto certain decisions or to refuse to participate in decision making. Representativeness is still a key source of legitimacy, as is the representatives' accountability to the partially autonomous units. Cox and King (1985) describe state legislatures as confederated systems. Other examples might include so-called "holding company" agencies, such as the U.S. Department of Health and Human Services and the now defunct Housing and Home Finance Administration (HHFA). HHFA, the predecessor of the Department of Housing and Urban Development, had several subunits (for instance, the Federal Housing and Urban Renewal administrations) that were virtually independent actors, subject only to nonbinding "coordination" by HHFA's head. Similarly, "garbage can mergers," which join organizations with largely unrelated missions and jurisdictions, may resemble confederations: the component units continue their past activities, seemingly oblivious to their new partners (see, e.g., Hult, 1987).

System Dynamics

How might these political systems develop in organizations? Part of the explanation may lie in the balance of values that designers, overseers, or members wish organizations to reflect. Where strict accountability to external actors is paramount, command-oriented systems may be indicated. Again, we can return to NASA: one reason for the mounting numbers of rules following the *Challenger* disaster may be the growing external demands that the agency be tied more closely to elected officials.

In addition, the networks in which organizations are embedded may influence their political systems. Organizations that are permeable to and dependent upon external actors may take on some of the features of those actors in order to ease interaction. Newman (1980) notes, for instance, that collectivist organizations often grow more like command systems over time as they try to cope with external pressures (cf. Ferguson, 1984, pp. 73, 211; Rothschild & Whitt, 1986, p. 69). Thus, some state and local agencies, as well as many private groups, refuse federal grants, contending that to "play the granting game" (Newman, 1980, p. 160) would mean following involved rules and adopting more hierarchical decision processes. More generally, William Scott concludes that a dominant societal ideology favors a narrowly defined "rationality" that emphasizes efficiency. A "system of organization which has both the form and spirit of representative government could not conform to the rational imperative," and hence would not long survive (1969, p. 52).

Similar dynamics may take place *within* organizations. It often is very difficult for subunits with political norms that diverge from those of other units to maintain their distinctiveness. Research units, for example, typically are staffed by professionals who strongly prefer and work best in more collectivist settings. Yet superiors in a largely command-oriented organization may not understand or be willing to tolerate such deviance; members of other subunits may consider the differences to be unfair or illegitimate. The solution may be either to insist on norms consistent with the rest of the organization or to isolate the deviant subunit—for example, by locating it away from the rest of the organization—in order to protect its integrity and to minimize friction with the rest of the organization.

Strong clientele groups may encourage pluralist or confederated arrangements by interjecting competing external interests into organizational political systems. Thus, legislatures are often subject to the centrifugal pulls of committees and the constituencies to which they respond (cf. Cox & King, 1985, p. 21). When the Department of Housing and Urban Development (HUD) was created in 1965, it became the arena for intense disputes over the proper direction for federal urban policy, in part as the confederated units of its predecessor, the HHFA, lost their vetoes over agency decisions. Former Public Housing Administration officials and their supporters among local public housing professionals squared off against the staff of the Federal Housing Administration (with mortgage bankers and the construction industry in their corner) over the appropriate balance between federal low-income housing and federal loans for middle-class homes. By the late 1960s, however, HUD grew less open to and dependent upon these strong external groups. The department also seemed to evolve from a pluralist political system to more of a command-oriented organization: Secretary Robert Weaver forcefully articulated and pursued a new federal role in urban affairs, one that went beyond an emphasis on physical redevelopment and servicing various constituencies to stress the social welfare of city residents (Hult, 1987).

Consideration of permeability and dependence also allows us to formulate more general expectations about the configuration of power in organizations and about the nature of their political systems. When permeability is high, power will flow to those in position to control needed resources from the larger environment (Pfeffer & Salancik, 1978). As NASA fell from its favored position in Washington after the success of the Apollo mission to the moon, those in the agency who were skilled at lobbying Congress and the White House and at gaining favorable attention from the news media grew in influence (Trento & Trento, 1987). When permeability is more moderate but external threat remains, power will flow to units that are able to buffer the organization from external pressure (M. Meyer, 1979, ch. 4). As we have noted, more careful judicial scrutiny of rule making has led to a rise in prominence within agencies of offices of general counsel and those with legal training. Under conditions of low or declining permeability, external dependence becomes less important, and power will flow to units with control over internal resources (Crozier, 1964). Units with needed expertise will gain influence, while units serving as access points for external groups (such as the Office of Public Liaison in the Reagan White House) may be ignored or bypassed.

These expectations suggest how power may be distributed within organizations, indicating, for example, which interests in pluralist or corporatist organizations might be most influential. They also may help explain shifts from one type of political system to another. For instance, when an organization is permeable to and dependent upon outside actors, and conflict becomes polarizing, the organization may move from a pluralist configuration with advocates for competing external interests to a confederation in which veto groups emerge. Alternatively, if top officials can shield the agency from external budget cuts, program limitations, or other threats, they also may be able to assume authoritative command or encourage more collectivist activity.

Desirable Organizational Political Systems

Offering prescriptions about organizational political systems is even more problematical than suggesting the most desirable governance structure or network. The difficulty is not simply that overall political patterns and dynamics in organizations are harder to influence; it is also that they reflect and must respond to numerous and diverse expectations. The legitimacy of entire organizational political systems is likely to entail more than the expectation that decisions meet criteria of bureaucratic rationality, representativeness, and accountability. One also may demand, for example, that government agencies respect the rights of those inside and outside the organization and in general make decisions without disastrous consequences. Moreover, while both internal and external ideologies provide support for more command-oriented polities, the fragmented national political system, with its plethora of institutional actors and interest groups, encourages more pluralist, corporatist, and even confederated arrangements.

For us, a collectivist organization, with its emphasis on equality and broad participation rights, is initially the most attractive type of political system. Certainly, it would seem to be so from the standpoint of most participants. Yet the size and complexity of most government organizations (though perhaps not, for example, schools or some local social service agencies) make it an unrealistic alternative (e.g., Rothschild & Whitt, 1986, p. 92). For many pressing policy problems, collectivist organizations would probably hinder bureaucratic rationality, making necessary expertise difficult to acquire and emphasize, and decision closure potentially hard to reach. Even more important, in the United States, collectivist government organizations would likely be seen as neither legitimate nor fully accountable.

Nevertheless, some of the desirable features of collectivist organizations—their more open decision making and insistence on fuller participation by members—might be incorporated in other kinds of political systems. For example, more collegial governance structures and team-oriented networks could be introduced into the system. Such measures arguably would enhance both bureaucratic rationality and representativeness by increasing the range and diversity of information and analysis available to decision makers. Accountability could be maintained both by including elected officials or their agents in decision making and by emphasizing the responsibility of participants for their actions. As we shall see, collegial structures and team networks could also enhance the quality of members' citizenship in the organization.

These sorts of changes might be made in any of the noncollectivist types of organizational polity. However, they seem most compatible with pluralist and corporatist systems, which hold open the possibility of (though they do not require) diffused influence. Of course, whether such shifts are possible or would be deemed legitimate given the pulls of hierarchy, bureaucracy, and command-oriented polities must remain open to question.

Ultimately, we must fall back upon a contingency approach to the question of desirable polities. The "best" form of organizational political system is a function of task, environment, and relevant ideologies inside and outside the organization. It likely will vary from one agency to another, across governmental levels, and among national political systems and cultures.

ORGANIZATIONAL CITIZENSHIP

Thinking about different political arrangements in organizations inevitably brings us to the role of individual organizational "citizens" and points to the implications of various organizational political systems for the rights and responsibilities of their members. We immediately confront the difficulty, however, of determining exactly what "organizational citizenship" might encompass. Citizenship is a slippery notion. According to the *Dictionary of American Government and Politics*, it refers to the "rules of what a citizen might do . . . , must do . . . , and can refuse to do" (Shafritz, 1988, p. 95). Morris Janowitz, drawing on Aristotle, observes that citizenship involves a "rough balance between rights and obligations in order to make possible the shared process of ruling and being ruled" (1980, p. 3; cf. Mead, 1986, p. 7).

But what, exactly, is the possible content of these benefits and duties? Recent political philosophy provides relatively little to build upon. In the United States, the struggles over McCarthyism and the pitched battles over Vietnam and civil rights so tainted the idea of citizenship and loaded it with such diverse connotations that many political theorists seem to have abandoned it altogether. Nonetheless, probing the characteristics of organizational citizenship evidently is crucial to understanding differences among organizations and to thinking about the rights and responsibilities of their members. An account of organizational citizenship also may serve as the foundation for designing government organizations that better serve both their members and the public.

The Meaning of Citizenship in Organizations

Following Daniel Katz, we contend that "[t]o be a member of an organization is to be a citizen in that community" (1964, p. 139).[1] The *grounds* (B. Barber, 1984, p. 218), or basis, of organizational citizenship minimally involves the economic contract between employer and employee. For many individuals, however, membership in an organization will entail more than that; like citizens of nation-states, they may share common beliefs or a commitment to common processes or ends. Government employees, for example, often are deeply committed to the mission of their agency, whether that mission is to deliver social services (e.g., Aberbach & Rockman, 1976), preserve the nation's forests (Kaufman, 1960), oversee executive branch agencies (Walker, 1986), or maintain military preparedness. Civil servants evidently also understand and accept the limits of their authority as unelected officials in a representative system of government (e.g., R. Cole & Caputo, 1979).

Defined by organizational boundaries, organizational citizens share particular governance structures and "subjective perceptions and expectations . . . about correct political action" (Pranger, 1968, p. 11). The attributes and quality of citizenship likely vary across organizations and among members of the same organization. Although citizenship is thus a complex and multifaceted concept, two aspects seem especially relevant for discussion here: the extent and nature of member participation in organizational decision making, and the demarcation between the public and private realms. (For a related discussion at the level of nation-states, see Roelofs, 1957.) We will first explore how these notions help us in analyzing citizenship in organizations and then discuss their normative implications.

Participation in organizational decision making. When thinking about citizenship in nation-states, scholars frequently zero in on *participation* and examine the roles people play in governance. In the United States, for example, political analysts explore the extent to which various kinds of people vote, campaign, contribute money to interest groups, or write letters to members of Congress. Organization theorists have devoted considerable attention to participation in organizations, investigating its effects on organizational performance and employee satisfaction (see, e.g., the ninety-one studies analyzed in Cotton et al., 1988). As these dependent variables suggest, however, most scholars focus on participation's contribution to the organization rather than its impact on organizational members as people (instead of simply as employees). Even proponents of "workplace democracy" often emphasize the protection of employee rights and en-

---

1 This usage differs from that of, for example, Dennis Organ (1988), who defines "organizational citizenship behavior" more narrowly and prescriptively: it is "individual behavior that is discretionary, not directly or explicitly recognized by the formal reward system, and that in the aggregate promotes the effective functioning of the organization" (p. 4).

hancement of their interests rather than the volume and character of their participation in organizational decision making (Mason, 1982, p. 152; Pateman, 1975). Moreover, except for the short-lived efforts by advocates of a New Public Administration, few have paid systematic attention to the possibilities of member participation in *public* agencies (but see Bernstein, 1988; Nurick, 1985; Patchen, 1976; Warwick, 1975).

Still, the notion of organizational citizens as participants in organizational governance is at least implicit in much work in democratic theory. Alexis de Tocqueville, for example, expected the family, religious bodies, voluntary associations, and by extension, the workplace (according to Bellah et al., 1985, p. 212) to fill the gap between individual and state by providing forums for active participation. Similarly, drawing on the works of Jean Jacques Rousseau, John Stuart Mill, and G. D. H. Cole, Carole Pateman (1970) argues for the significance of a "participatory society" as the basis for "participatory democracy" in nation-states. From these perspectives, organizational participation is important *instrumentally* as a means of fostering democracy in the larger political system and *intrinsically* for its effects on the self-esteem and sense of efficacy of individual participants (cf. R. Denhardt, 1984, pp. 121–23; Mason, 1982).

Clearly, however, what participation means in concrete organizations can vary markedly. As we have already mentioned, "participation rights"—specifications of who may participate when, where, and how—are shaped by prevailing governance structures and networks, organizational ideologies, and external constraints and expectations.

More formally, participation in organizational decision making may vary along several dimensions (such as those outlined in Cotton et al., 1988; Mason, 1982, pp. 154–55; and Nagel, 1987, p. 161). The first dimension taps whether participation is direct or indirect, that is, whether decisions are made by organizational members themselves or by representatives or agents acting on the members' behalf. Employees might vote, for example, on whether they want to have the option of working flexible hours ("flextime"); alternatively, union representatives may decide whether to approach management with such a demand.

A second dimension concerns whether participation is formal or informal. This dimension gets at the extent to which formal governance structures exist for involving members in decision making. In some settings, there are clearly specified routines for gathering employee input or allowing workers to express grievances and suggest ideas; in other cases, more informal interactions among members serve the same purposes.

A third dimension is the organizational level at which participation takes place. Members might be involved in decisions affecting only their own work, the work of all of those in their subunit, or the activities and operations of the entire organization.

A fourth dimension is the scope of the decisions that members may influence. Are they involved in all decisions, in only those decisions directly affecting workers, or in overall policy decisions?

The final dimension concerns the extent of members' influence. In some instances, members might all have an equal vote on decisions; other times, some might exercise an absolute veto. In still other cases, organizational members merely may have access to key decision makers, perhaps submitting written assessments of proposals or seeking to exercise informal persuasion.

These dimensions provide a way of untangling the complex notion of participation rights and of noting variations between organizations and among organizational members. In particular, the political systems we introduced earlier in the chapter differ dramatically in the degree and nature of members' involvement in decision making (see table 8). Employees in command-oriented polities, for example, probably participate less than those in collectivist settings, although informal governance structures may fill some of the gap. Moreover, in the former, there are likely to be significant differences among members in their access and contributions to decision making. Collectivist polities, in contrast, typically place a high premium on political equality; even so, differences in members' motivation and expertise may lead to variations in their actual influence over decisions. In more pluralist polities and corporatist settings, levels of influence and scope of involvement likely differ with the distribution and dynamics of power among internal players; most members may participate indirectly, leaving negotiation and alliance-building to representatives. Confederated organizations may have members who consider themselves citizens of subunits more than of the organization as a whole and so confine their participation to internal subunit matters.

In addition, as our discussion of governance structures and networks highlighted, participation rights can vary dramatically within organizations. This in turn may introduce significant differences among individuals in the nature of their involvement in organizational governance as well as variations for the same individual in different decision settings. For example, an agency's congressional liaison officer, working in a bargaining network, may spend considerable time developing legislative proposals with other agency officials, OMB employees, members of the White House staff, members of Congress and their staffs, and agency constituents. Meanwhile, a policy analyst in the same organization might interact in a collegial-consensual structure with professional peers in his or her subunit while also being subject to the demands and constraints of bureaucratic networks in the agency.

The distinction between public and private. A second aspect of citizenship concerns the part of an individual's life that the state or an organization is concerned with and seeks to influence. In the context of organizations,

TABLE 8 Nature of Participation in Organizational Polities

| Polity | Direct or Indirect | Formal or Informal | Dimensions of Participation | | | Scope of Decision |
			Organizational Level	Extent of Member Influence		
Command	Neither	Formal	Authority flows down, information up	High at top, declines as one moves down chain of command		May be street-level discretion
Collectivist	Direct preferred; also indirect	Both	All levels	Equal input; influence varies with personal resources		All decisions
Pluralist	Indirect	Both	Variable, inter-subgroup dominates	Depends on influence distribution		Decisions involving subgroup interests
Corporatist	Indirect	Both	Variable, inter-subunit dominates	Depends on influence distribution		Decisions involving functional interests
Confederated[a]	Indirect	Formal	Organization level	Subunit veto		Decisions affecting confederation

[a]Participation within subunits may vary on all of these dimensions; table entries refer to interaction among subunits.

the private realm becomes that which is not absorbed into the employment relationship (cf. Redford, 1969, p. 157), the public sphere that which is relevant to the organization (Mead, 1986, p. 242).

One might array organizations along a spectrum of degree of involvement in their members' lives. The least involved organizations, where the sphere of privacy is the largest, would be those in which citizenship is grounded solely in economic exchange: employees perform the organization's work in return for pay, and they can end the relationship rather than do work that violates their sense of values. At the opposite extreme are jobs in which individuals accord "total commitment" to organizations. This sort of relationship may be most commonly associated with cults and some religious groups, but it also may surface for at least short periods in other social movement organizations (Zald & Ash, 1966), such as those surrounding abortion and civil rights. Government agencies with mandates to protect the environment, intercept drug shipments, prosecute insider traders, or fight employment discrimination similarly may foster such commitment and attract the already committed, especially early in the life cycle of the organization (see, e.g., Downs, 1967).

Between these extremes are organizational efforts to inculcate shared values and a sense of mission through such means as formal training sessions and employee rotation through several jobs. Providing on-site child care and testing for drug and alcohol use are among the ways employers seek to ensure that "private" demands and problems do not interfere with more "public" responsibilities. Government employees typically have more restrictions placed upon their private activities than do their private sector counterparts (cf. Mosher, 1968). The Hatch Act, for instance, constrains the political activities of federal civil servants. Many government employees also are subject to loyalty and security checks and to conflict-of-interest laws.

As with participation, organizations are likely to differ in their demarcation of the public and private realms. Of the types of organizational polity we have discussed, collectivist political systems may routinely demand the most of individuals, in part because the often more intense and extensive participation breeds deeper commitment and requires significant expenditure of time and energy (see, e.g., Rothschild & Whitt, 1986; Rothschild-Whitt, 1979). Command-oriented organizations sometimes insist on intense commitment, as symbolized by particular types of behavior; the military, for example, not only specifies dress and hair length, but also restricts fraternization between enlisted personnel and officers and tries to deny entry to gays. Yet a command polity can be just as compatible with relationships based primarily on economic exchange.

Corporatist and pluralist polities probably fall in the intermediate range. They are likely to be characterized by at least a moderate level of commitment to the organization as an arena in which subgroup interests are pursued and negotiated; in turn, some level of identification both with particular subgroups and with the organization as a whole may be expected. Because of more stable patterns of interaction, commitment to subgroups and decision-making partners probably is greater in corporatist polities. Confederated political systems, in contrast, seem apt to have a more restricted public sphere; their component units, however, might make higher demands on their members than does the organization as a whole.

In addition, organizations may draw the lines between public and private differently depending on the individual and his or her responsibilities and position in the organization. For example, within certain limits, the attire and values of clerical personnel may make little difference to organizational superiors, who pay much more attention to professional employees or those dealing directly with the public. Similarly, drug testing may be mandated only for those in "sensitive" positions, such as air traffic controllers or CIA analysts. Collegial-consensual structures, with their emphasis on mutual exploration of goals or technologies, may demand that participants reveal more about their values, intentions, and uncertainties than hierarchical structures that require only prespecified responses.

Assessing Organizational Citizenship

Clearly, even our brief discussion of two aspects of organizational citizenship raises complex normative issues. What should citizenship in government organizations entail? Like citizenship in nation-states, the concept of organizational citizenship directs attention to both rights and obligations.

Rights of organizational citizens. A minimum notion of organizational citizenship might focus upon the rights of all members (cf. Katz, 1964). In agencies of the U.S. Government, the Civil Service system is the basic instrument for spelling out rights, such as protection against arbitrary demotion and dismissal and provision for appeal. Over time, these rights have expanded to include the results of labor-management negotiations, yielding, for example, pregnancy leaves. Scott (1969, p. 51) goes somewhat farther, arguing that "citizens of organizations" should have the right not only to appeal decisions affecting them but also to "participate in legislative affairs where rights are formulated."

Citizenship might be even more encompassing. Philip Green (1985, p. 206) contends, for example, that in the larger political system the rights of "democratic citizens" include "participation in participatory or representative politics, freedom of intellectual and spiritual expression, freedom of association, and completely open government."

To what extent can such rights be extended to the workplace? Participation poses a particularly thorny issue. Proponents of the New Public Administration in the early 1970s worried that by denying meaningful member participation in organizational decision making, command-oriented public agencies stunted the personal development of their employees, stifling their creativity and sense of purpose (e.g., Marini, 1971). This had negative consequences for individuals and society alike. Public employees may not have felt responsible for their actions, being content instead to follow orders and shunt blame elsewhere (cf. Merton, 1940). This kind of moral numbness, critics argued, contributed to U.S. involvement in Vietnam, to demeaning treatment of welfare recipients, and to slow responses by government to charges of racial discrimination. More recently, in a study of local bureaucrats, Judith Gruber found that none described themselves as "public officials" or saw any direct connection between their work and the operation of a democratic national political system (1987, pp. 101–2).

Yet to address such charges by providing for more participation in decision making poses other problems. Chief among them is the question of accountability: granting lower civil servants more influence over important decisions may threaten the ability of elected officials to guide policy making:

> [D]emocracy within administration, if carried to the full, raises a logical dilemma in its relation to political democracy. All public organizations are presumed to have been established and to operate for public purposes . . . They are authorized, legitimated, empowered, and usually supported by authorities for broad purposes initially determined outside of themselves. To what extent, then, should "insiders," the officers and employees, be able to modify their purposes, their organizational arrangements, and their means of support? (Mosher, 1968, pp. 18–19, his emphases)

Might government organizations, through participation, foster among their members a sense of personal responsibility for their actions that would be an acceptable complement to reduced "overhead democracy"? The question provokes ongoing controversy (see, e.g., Burke, 1986; Redford, 1969, p. 178).

Bureaucratic rationality might suffer as well. Increased participation may hamper decision closure and in some cases reduce the significance accorded to input by experts (e.g., Rothschild & Whitt, 1986, p. 139).

Furthermore, on some occasions seeking enhanced participation may be inconsistent with the prescriptions of a problem contingency approach to organizational design. Neither hierarchy nor adjudicative governance structures, for example, provide for very widespread or influential member participation; market structures are more open but by definition do not require or formally encourage participation. Similarly, bureaucratic networks are characterized by inequality; in consultative networks, decision makers may choose not to tap the opinions of many organizational members. Such governance structures and networks may well be appropriate to their decision settings even though, to the extent that participation is valued as an end in itself, they hamper its realization. Still, as we shall see, there may be ways to increase participation that stop short of the "democracy within administration" that worries Mosher.

Just as complicated are issues involving the distinction between public and private. On the one hand, as the advocates of the New Public Administration suggested, increased member involvement in organizational activities may reduce alienation and heighten employees' sense of self-worth as well as their commitment to the agency's work. For government organizations this effect would be particularly salutary, for it might well mean enhanced motivation to serve the public. On the other hand, an expanded public sphere within organizations raises the specter of "totalitarian" organizations with automatons for workers. Individualism and diversity, and hence liberty (D. Thompson, 1987, pp. 124–25), may decline as organizations seek control over the extra-employment activities of their members. Should an employee be fired when a drug test uncovers evidence of weekend pot smoking? Should gays be excluded from employment as school teachers, foreign service officers, or CIA analysts? Meanwhile, organizational efforts to foster shared values may work against equal access to jobs, as is apparently the case in many Japanese firms (Ouchi, 1980) and at the higher levels of U.S. corporations (Kanter, 1977). Such attempts also may stifle the dissent that more participatory structuring tries to encourage. Like the complex issue of participation, the question of how to encourage "public-spirited" organizational citizenship without interfering with privacy deserves fuller contemplation and discussion.

Obligations of organizational citizens. The rights of citizens typically are taken to entail corresponding obligations (e.g., Janowitz, 1980). Although modern discussions of citizenship in nation-states often give greater prominence to citizens' rights than to their duties (Janowitz, 1980; Mead, 1986, p. 257), the reverse seems to be true in organizations, especially government agencies. Nevertheless, the possible responsibilities of organizational members are worthy of attention, perhaps particularly as one explores according them more meaningful rights.

Even the most minimal notion of organizational citizenship—economic exchange between employer and employee—implies the obligations of both to live up to the terms of the contract. Employees, for example, are expected not to shirk their responsibilities or otherwise defraud the employer. As the citizenship relationship becomes more complex, duties multiply. Thus, enhanced participation rights would appear to carry with them the obligations to participate actively and in good faith (rather than, for example, hiding or distorting information or evaluations). While command organizations might reasonably demand only that members follow the chain of command when confronting a problem, collectivist polities are based in part on the expectation that members will be energetic, persistent, and constructively critical participants in decision making. Confederated political systems likely would place more importance on involvement in subunit activities. Members of pluralist and corporatist polities bear responsibility for expressing and pursuing subgroup interests in the larger organization. In pluralist systems, the range and fluidity of those interests will be broader, requiring members to be constantly alert for nonroutine opportunities to press their interests.

Different polities also seem to point to varying obligations to the organization as a whole. In some command polities, members may not need to share the organization's overall goals and values if they observe the rules for attaining organizational objectives; the danger, of course, is displacement of organizational goals and the elevation of means to ends (Merton, 1940). Yet in other command polities, such as combat units or the priesthood, the expectation of goal commitment is unusually high. In collectivist organizations, obligations are strong: since members are roughly equal participants, presumably with significant (though not necessarily equal) influence over decisions, they become responsible for acting in accordance with the values and objectives of the organization and following collective decisions. Among the risks here is "groupthink," a growing organizational incapacity to seriously consider diverse and conflicting views and to adapt to changing environments (Janis, 1972). Meanwhile, members of corporatist and pluralist political systems are obligated to take as authoritative the negotiated outcomes resulting from the interplay of subgroup interests, just as members of confederated organizations must live in a system of subunit vetoes.

The demarcation between public and private in organizations also appears to entail obligations. As the public realm expands, so does a member's duty to share more of the organization's values and goals, or else to leave. Heightened, too, of course, is the threat of a "totalitarian" organization. At the same time, organizational members arguably have a responsibility not to interfere in matters falling into the "private" sphere. They may be obligated, for example, to refrain from formally or informally pressuring other members to behave in particular (not organizationally relevant) ways or to adopt certain political stances.

Balancing rights and obligations. Finding the "correct" balance between the rights and obligations of organizational citizens is at best problematical. As our discussion has suggested, the tradeoffs and potential problems are numerous.

Still, we would contend that, in government organizations, more consideration needs to be given to expanding the participation rights—and hence the duties and expectations—of organizational members. As we contended earlier, demands for accountability to elected officials, the enormous size of many government agencies, and the complexity of much of what government does make collectivist polities and "organizational democracy" unreasonable goals. Nevertheless, structures might permit "partial participation" (Pateman, 1970, p. 70), in which not all participate directly and the final power to decide rests with another party. Especially at the level of task performance, partial participation seems both feasible and desirable. For example, members' involvement in decision making might be increased by formal access to and information about decision making at higher levels of government agencies, coupled with more informal consultation among organizational members and more participatory structuring of activities closer to workers' actual tasks—for example, through collegial governance structures or networks encouraging bargaining, consultation, or confrontation (see, too, Mason, 1982, pp. 158–71). Additionally, though more systematic data are needed, available evidence for the private sector suggests that more "democratic management" brings "effectively higher levels of worker commitment and solidarity, and thus can often be turned into a labor productivity and profitability advantage" (Rothschild & Whitt, 1986, p. 167).

There have been some successful efforts to increase participation in public organizations. The Tennessee Valley Authority (TVA) institutionalized a "cooperative conference" program in the early 1940s to encourage labor-management collaboration (see, e.g., Nurick, 1985; Patchen, 1976). Designed to supplement collective bargaining, conferences with equal numbers of labor and management representatives were established in each workplace; these groups met monthly, often for several hours at a time. They made decisions (by consensus) on a range of issues (with the critical exception of matters subject to collective bargaining); management, however, retained the final responsibility for accepting and executing decisions. At least in the early to mid-1960s, the conference system not only led to increased acceptance of work changes among employees but also heightened workers' perceived influence at the work-group level and in the organization as a whole (Patchen, 1976, p. 169). Nurick (1985) found some deterioration in the utility of the conferences by the mid-1970s. Yet, he also reported their revitalization in one subunit through the temporary introduction of a Quality of Work Life Committee. This committee was authorized to discuss all issues, and its establishment resulted both in heightened member participation in decision making and in efforts to resolve several technological and structural problems.

In New York City, the Department of Sanitation has established twenty-two Field Operations Improvement Committees. These committees have both labor and management representatives as well as staff analysts. They have been instrumental in making important internal policy changes, such as the creation of " 'profit centers' in the central repair shop (comparing the cost of activities to the city with the cost of the same goods or services on the outside); replacement of work standards with performance standards; [and] major cost avoidance in landfill operations approaching $1 million annually" (Holzer, 1988, p. 42). In addition, Labor-Management Committees in the city's fifty-nine sanitation districts bring together union officials, the district and assistant borough supervisors, and representatives of professional groups inside and outside the department to discuss both productivity and job quality issues. The participants consider these groups to be successful (Holzer, 1988, p. 44).

Similarly, some elementary and secondary schools in the United States are experimenting with teacher-administration cooperation, even though the schools remain enmeshed in a larger bureaucratic network (Bernstein, 1988; cf. Chubb, 1988). Pilot programs in communities such as Pittsburgh, Cincinnati, and Dade County, Florida, bring together elected teacher representatives and principals to make decisions on budget allocations, class size, curriculum development, textbook selection, and other issues. The preliminary indications are that this sort of "cooperative management" reduces internal conflict, improves the quality of teaching, and makes teachers feel increasingly like contributing and influential members of the institution.

These kinds of enhanced participation opportunities might increase bureaucratic rationality by interjecting diverse information and analyses into decision making. They also could improve representativeness. Since lower-level agency workers are more likely to be minorities, women, and from varying class backgrounds, at least potentially they hold points of view different from those of more senior officials. Street-level bureaucrats might be expected to offer the perspectives of clients and constituents.

Enhanced participation rights bring corresponding obligations—to participate actively and in good faith, and to accept the resulting decisions. These duties might in turn increase accountability by making responsibilities more visible and by increasing members' commitment to the carrying out of decisions and to the organization and its missions (as suggested by the TVA and New York Department of Sanitation experiments and by teacher-administrator cooperation). At least as important, such changes would move organizations toward treating government workers as capable and worthwhile human beings, as citizens inside as well as outside the workplace.

It remains an open question whether such partial participation is sufficient to overcome the pressures of traditionally command-oriented organizations or to strengthen the links between the work of government employees and the larger political system. Indeed, one may well be pessimistic about the likelihood of major advances in member participation in organizational governance. Our discussion of the persistence of hierarchy indicates that both external opposition and internal ideologies pose significant barriers to the enhancement of participation in government agencies. TVA's cooperative conferences died after the Reagan administration came to power and labor-management conflict escalated. Moreover, organizational size appears to constrain the extent and significance of member participation in decision making (e.g., Rothschild & Whitt, 1986, p. 92; Warwick, 1975, p. 202). Still, the possibility of introducing more participatory governance structures in government organizations seems worthy of further exploration.

Our consideration of citizenship returns us to some of the challenges of organizing laid out in chapter 1. When should individual values and goals be subordinated to organizational purposes? If organizations are intended to pursue collective ends, who speaks for the "collectivity"? These questions are far more than matters for armchair philosophers. They lie at the base of many employee demands for greater participation in decision making and of often wrenching decisions about whether to criticize superiors, to leak information to the press or a sympathetic member of Congress, or to resign in protest. Nor is there agreement on whether public employees should bear heavier responsibilities and have less autonomy in these matters than their counterparts in the private sector.

That such thorny issues may never be resolved should not obscure their importance. Indeed, the question of citizenship ultimately may be the most compelling reason for thinking about organizations as polities. Viewing organizations as primarily control systems or natural systems reduces their members to objects, manipulated either by internal demands for compliance or by external forces. From the polity perspective, in contrast, organizational members are also *subjects*, worthy of concern independently of their contribution to organizational performance. Explicitly considering individuals increases the complexity of analysis and may make it harder to attain some organization-level objectives. But it also places in sharp relief a fundamental point: organizations as such are mere artifacts, constructs we use to talk about collective efforts. Human beings are not.

CHAPTER NINE

The Challenge of Organizational Design

Redesigning organizations is like "repairing a truck while it continues to travel at top speed down an interstate highway" (Mackenzie, 1986, p. 11). The prospects for success are tenuous, the potential for calamity great. And still reformers urge the redesign of public organizations, and decision makers insist on attempting it, for the promise of improving governmental performance is tantalizing and the risks of inaction loom large. After all, riding in a fast-moving but defective truck is not an enticing prospect.

The image of organizations as polities and the governance model that flows from it offer a distinct vantage point from which to view these efforts at redesign and to propose alternatives. They also reorient our more general understanding of public organizations and the processes of policy making and implementation.

We begin exploring the implications of our theoretical ideas by recalling some of the basic assumptions that underlie the "politically informed" perspective this book has introduced. These premises are not obviously or necessarily correct, and one's willingness to "buy into" the theory as a whole may be based upon one's acceptance or rejection of its foundations.

Our most critical assumption is that organization matters. Human beings, in trying to pool their efforts in order to achieve collective goals, can adopt a variety of organizational schemes. Along with many others who have sought to theorize about organizations, we believe that the particular form of organization that is chosen is likely to have important consequences for the ability of people to attain their goals—as well as other, unanticipated effects. Conversely, we are not persuaded by those who argue that organizational design, or reorganization plans, are important only as symbols or illusions.

The assertion that organization matters leads naturally (though not inevitably) to something like the notion of organizations as "rational tools." If design properties have consequences, we ought to be able to understand and anticipate them. We can then develop theories of design that enable us to choose those structural characteristics that will both increase the probability of attaining desired *outcomes* and have desirable *process* characteristics. We have called these efforts at design and redesign "organization policy." This simple faith has undergirded and inspired generations of public administration scholars and practitioners, reformers and conservers alike. However, formulating and implementing organizational policy are obviously not easy. While we may reject in principle the assertion that organizational structure is a non-issue, we have to concede that the track record of designers generally is not impressive. If it seems clear that structure matters at least some of the time, scholars have not done very well at developing a capacity to predict and direct its consequences. So far, theory has not been adequate.

This failure brings us to our second basic point, and back to elephants. What one "sees" in an organization depends upon how and where one looks. Although this applies both to structures and to their consequences, our focus here is upon the former. The view typically held by reformers represents, in effect, one blind person's version of the pachyderm. Ours provides another. Neither captures the whole beast. But if the traditional model—grounded in the metaphor of organizations as control systems—has not proven as useful as many had hoped, it is reasonable to consider an alternative. It is in that spirit that we have proposed the image of the organization as polity and the governance model. We have suggested that the design and operation of public organizations raise issues of politics more than those of control. The governance model grows out of this understanding and leads to one version of organization policy.

By beginning with the assumption that politics is central to public organizations, rather than illegitimate within or to be excluded from them, we have placed ourselves in a broad tradition of constitutional design. We are in a sense working on the same kind of problem as that faced by, for example, the framers of the United States Constitution: the design of *political* systems. In much the same spirit that animated the founders, governance analysis is an experiment. It assumes politics *in* rather than *out* of organizations and follows where that assumption might lead.

The governance model produces at least three important kinds of insights. First, it helps analysts see things they might otherwise have missed. This point is best demonstrated by example; the next section returns to our initial case study, the explosion of the space shuttle *Challenger*. Second, a politically informed analysis of public organizations reveals a great deal about theory construction in public administration and the even more general issue of relating public administration theory to a broader institutional analysis of American government. The second section of the chapter will address these issues. Third, the governance model directs attention to prescription; we conclude by exploring the implications of the model for the development of organization policy.

CHALLENGER REVISITED

Many people have tried to make sense of the *Challenger* disaster and have searched for ways to reduce the probability of a similar accident, among them the Rogers Commission, members of Congress, White House staffers, NASA officials, journalists, and average citizens. Not surprisingly, their answers have been diverse.

Similarly, the views of organizations we have surveyed offer differing diagnoses of the problems at NASA and correspondingly different pre-scriptions. An understanding of organizations as control systems, for ex-ample, likely would lead to an emphasis on insufficient headquarters control of field space centers. In this view, Washington staff paid too much attention to lobbying Congress and the White House for more money, defending NASA against encroachment by the military space program, calming angry commercial customers, and trying to defuse increasingly critical media coverage. Too little time was left for enforcing paperwork requirements and ensuring that formal communication channels were open and that people at the top knew of difficulties in the field. These problems were complicated by the absence of strong, credible leadership and by rivalries and infighting (pathologies also identified by the political arena model).

The prescriptions of control-oriented analysts likely would be equally clear. Most important from this perspective, NASA officials needed to work to make hierarchical structures and bureaucratic networks function as they are intended to. As we have noted, the agency's responses have largely been along these lines.

In contrast, proponents of the natural system perspective might well take the position that there was little NASA could have done to avoid its problems. Simply put, the once proud space agency was overwhelmed by its environment—besieged by a hounding press and by hostile constituents and overseers, and operating under severe resource constraints. Under these circumstances, compelling prescriptions are hard to come by. It seems doubtful that the agency could buffer itself from outside influences as effectively as it did in the 1960s, when, for example, the "safety first" rule led to many delays even when there was heavy pressure to stay on schedule (cf. Trento & Trento, 1987, p. 28).

Unlike either the control or natural systems perspectives, the gover-nance model would focus more explicitly on NASA's political structuring and the appropriateness of that structuring to the conditions the agency faced. Chapter 1 suggested that the space shuttle program was beset by considerable uncertainty and controversy over both goals and technologies. The problem contingency approach that we have outlined indicates that the hierarchical structures and bureaucratic networks that emerged in NASA through the 1970s and 1980s—which control analysts probably would advocate strengthening—did not match many of the agency's decision settings. Indeed, they probably contributed significantly to NASA's inability to base its decisions on the full range of available data, to include all relevant actors, and to fix responsibility for decisions. It is likely that hierarchy and bureaucracy both reflected and aggravated the space agency's misplaced "preference for short-term certainty" (Kettl, 1988, p. 147).

Previous chapters point to possible directions for organizational redesign. For example, throughout the shuttle's development, there seems to have been a need for more interaction among "professionals" (Romzek & Dubnick, 1987) and between experts in the space centers and top headquarters officials (Trento & Trento, 1987, p. 257). Hierarchical reporting procedures substituted for more probing discussions of problems. Among the results were the management isolation noted by the Rogers Commission and the evident failure to fully examine the many technical ambiguities and controversies. More appropriate might have been collegial-consensual structures encouraging exploration of technical uncertainties such as the sealing mechanism for the O-rings or the more general problem of assessing the risks associated with flying the shuttle. Collegial-competitive structures might have fostered a more thorough airing of conflicts over goals and technologies and more acceptable "quasi-resolutions," which might well have been less corrosive of agency morale and the credibility of top decision makers. Representation in these collegial groups would be a key issue: for example, slots for representatives of engineers from NASA and its contractors, the space centers, headquarters, scientists, line managers, and astronauts all seem indicated. Along similar lines, the Rogers Commission advocated placing representatives of a new NASA safety unit, mission operations, and astronauts on a "safety advisory panel" (U.S. Presidential Commission, 1986, p. 199). NASA's response was to name former astronaut Robert Crippen head of a "mission management team" whose twenty-four experts represented a range of specialties and were authorized to stop a launch (Dye, 1988, p. 30).

Different structuring also might have brought the competition among the field centers and the associated technical controversies more into the open. Confrontational networks might have brought representatives of the centers together, with headquarters officials serving as referees and final decision makers. In addition, units might have been created to champion other interests in these disputes. For instance, the Rogers Commission recommended establishment of an Office of Safety, Reliability, and Quality Assurance, whose head would report directly to the NASA Administrator

(U.S. Presidential Commission, 1986, p. 199). Others propose designating astronauts as "safety lobbyists" (Gormley & Peters, 1987).

The thrust of these sorts of prescriptions is that overall efforts to redesign NASA should be directed at moving it away from a command organization toward more of a corporatist political system. Ensuring participation rights for critical groups would enhance representativeness. It also would be likely to promote interaction among those with varying interests and expertise, thereby bolstering bureaucratic rationality by exposing decision makers to a broader range of information and analysis. Further, to the extent that top executives with final decision authority learned about risks and potential problems and actually oversaw decision making, they could more easily be held accountable for key decisions. The likely result would be greater legitimacy for NASA and its decisions. In addition, the commitment of NASA workers to the organization and their sense of involvement in and importance to its operation might be heightened; the quality of both organizational citizenship and task performance might improve as a consequence.

Clearly, however, as both the natural system and control system views recognize, many of the agency's problems stemmed from environmental pressures. NASA evidently was enmeshed in confrontational networks—involving the White House, Congress, commercial shuttle customers, and the military—in which the space agency typically was an ineffectual participant. Possibly needed was more constructive White House or congressional involvement in arbitrating disputes between NASA and the military, as well as efforts to upgrade NASA's access to policy decisions. Such a design—which calls for linked confrontational and appeals networks—seems appropriate given the high levels of goal and technical controversy. It might have encouraged fuller probing of these conflicts, with policy decisions made by elected officials or their agents. This exploration would have advanced bureaucratic rationality, while the involvement of elected officials would have maintained external accountability. Strengthening NASA's position in decision making would have promised the agency greater representation without necessarily leading to outcomes in its favor.

NASA's links with its contractors, though less threatening, showed the agency's weakness and dependence. Here, more confrontational relationships might have been useful. Decision making might have featured participation by contractors, scientific and safety officials from the agency, and, perhaps, independent experts with final decision authority reserved for top NASA officials. Such a structure might well have enhanced both bureaucratic rationality and accountability.

Although the governance model cannot guarantee that these design changes would have either helped avoid the *Challenger* accident or yielded improved agency performance, it does hold out the hope that structures, networks, and organizational political systems can be manipulated to improve the process of decision making and, perhaps, produce more desirable outcomes. The model also directs both analytical and evaluative attention to political structuring, which other views neglect.

TOWARD A THEORY OF PUBLIC INSTITUTIONS

If the governance model can provide insights beyond those supplied by the control and natural system perspectives, it enriches our understanding of public organizations. This potential brings us up against another problem that plagues theorists of public administration and students of American politics as a whole: the difficulty of integrating the study of public administration into the broader framework of the analysis of U.S. political institutions. The difficulty may stem in part from the failure of the Constitution to say much about public administration—an understandable omission, given the limited view of government prevalent in the eighteenth century. In any case, conventional discussions of separation of powers, checks and balances, and the Constitution as a very "conservative" system design often exclude executive agencies, independent boards and commissions, and the like. This exclusion is unfortunate, especially in view of the fact that many of these administrative institutions were, in effect, created by policy activists seeking to surmount some of the limitations of the constitutional system. Independent regulatory agencies, for instance, have been imbued with quasi-legislative, executive, and judicial powers in the recognition that effective policy implementation sometimes will require that these be used in concert, rather than distributed among competing actors.

The tendency to view public agencies as somehow off to the side of the main institutional show was long reinforced by the adoption, by both scholars and practitioners of public administration, of a strongly control-oriented image of executive branch organizations. Orthodox theory and civil service systems alike have insisted upon a dichotomy between "politics" and "administration," with the latter viewed entirely from the standpoint of efficiency and control (primarily by elected officials). Such a posture has been reinforced by the fear that any other understanding of the nature of public agencies might be inconsistent with the idea of democratic government.

Of course, as we have seen, a voluminous literature expressly challenges the notion of a dichotomy between politics and administration. Administrative activity of virtually all kinds has been shown again and again to be "politicized"—in every imaginable sense of that term. It is now commonplace to view the dichotomy as a great oversimplification, if not an outright fiction. Still, outside the realm of case studies, it has been difficult to make progress toward integrating public administration scholarship with the bulk of institutional analysis of the American system. This, we suspect, owes much to the fact that, however discredited the simple view of government agencies as control systems may be, scholars have lacked a systematic alternative to it. Works in the vein of Allison's (1971) examination of the Cuban Missile Crisis have come the closest, and they have been justly applauded. However, although these analyses have focused explicitly upon the political aspects of organizations, their model has been that of the political arena, with its attendant limitations to generalization.

It is here that governance analysis may point the way to further progress. In using the governance model to study organizations, we have advanced essentially the same evaluative criteria that one might use in looking at institutions such as Congress, the presidency, and the Supreme Court. We have argued for the analytical "partial autonomy" of public agencies as complex sets of governance structures; this view offers an alternative to seeing them simply as appendages to or consequences of external politics. At the same time, the concept of governance networks provides a conceptual tool for tracing the interrelationships and interdependencies among public agencies and between agencies and the rest of the institutional system. Thus, the understanding of organizational design as an intrinsically political, "constitutional" matter encourages us, and the idea of networks virtually compels us, to view public agencies in the context of other, explicitly political institutions.

This perspective has the further consequence of broadening our notion of legitimacy as it applies to executive branch agencies. The introduction of process values congruent with those employed in appraising the working of the "political" institutions forces us to consider matters beyond the question of whether administrators are responsive to elected officials. Concerns with bureaucratic rationality and representativeness, as well as accountability, are not new, of course, but focusing upon organizational governance heightens their salience and broadens their applicability. This may help bring public agencies into the charmed circle of legitimacy that we have drawn around the other institutions of government in the United States. The result may well be new enthusiasm for the sort of institutional experimentation within and among public agencies that the founders envisioned for the entire American system of governance.

ORGANIZATION POLICY

The analysis in this book has been, to a considerable extent, prescriptive. This is very much in the spirit of the image of organizations as control systems (though not of the natural systems view) and of the study of public (and private) management more generally. We have sought to address the practical problems of organizational design and redesign in a manner that incorporates and responds to the concerns advanced by the governance model. Our purposes have been to broaden the range of issues typically addressed by designers, to link them with concerns about policy making, and to suggest that design questions often transcend the boundaries of any particular organizational unit.

In advancing an alternative perspective on organizational design, our intent is scarcely to supplant all previous thought on the matter. Rather, by developing a coherent set of prescriptions derived from an image of organizations as polities, we seek to add to the total range of considerations that can and should be interjected into discussions of institutional design or redesign.

Some caveats are in order, however. First, it is clear that organizational design is not a panacea. Design, we have argued, can contribute to decision outcomes as it increases the likelihood of effective policy formulation and implementation. Yet organizational design is not the only determinant of outcomes, or even always the main one. Problems in the performance of public organizations need not be consequences of faulty design; nor can successes always be attributed to design excellence. Good people matter, too, probably at least as much as good structures. For example, NASA evidently suffered from White House politicking in naming its top decision makers; lower levels were plagued by poor worker morale. Structural changes might have affected these problems only marginally. Similarly, environmental factors may influence outcomes independently of structural design. In the *Challenger* case, government restrictions on asbestos (as a carcinogen) led to the abandonment of a special putty used to help seal the joints of solid rocket boosters; the replacement putty was less satisfactory and may have contributed to the explosion of the shuttle. Even so, when one considers process values as well as policy outcomes in judging organizational performance, it becomes clear that design—specifically, politically informed design—is an indispensable consideration.

As students of politics, though, we remain sensitive to the fact that the introduction of the polity metaphor may complicate organizational redesign in practice. After all, its main effect seems to be to introduce new evaluative standards on top of existing ones. Current design criteria, which stress efficiency and control, may not be fully adequate, but they are not wholly irrelevant either; certainly, we would not advocate their complete abandonment. Indeed, our criteria are not always antithetical to the traditional standards. We contend that the prevailing definition of efficiency is not wrong but rather too narrow for many circumstances; we urge adoption of the broader standard of bureaucratic rationality. Control and external accountability in many cases may be synonymous, though we believe that accountability extends beyond conventional notions of overhead democracy. The desirability of control and external accountability must be balanced against the benefits of acknowledging that public organizations are semiautonomous (but nevertheless responsible) policy-making institutions.

To the extent that we do advance novel standards, our analysis introduces potentially competing criteria by which structures or proposals for redesign may be analyzed and assessed. We anticipate that these criteria may enrich the evaluative repertoire of organization theorists and policy evaluators, even as they add complexity to their tasks.

Of course, solutions to problems of design and assessment will themselves be matters of political judgment. The design of public agencies should respond to a variety of factors: the nature of the problems or policy areas with which agencies deal, the values of citizens or their elected representatives, and the capacities of organizational members and of their constituents and overseers. As the governance model stresses, each of these is likely to be ambiguous and contested by those with compelling arguments and legitimate stakes in organizational outcomes.

A second caveat concerns the limitations of organization policy. Development of the theoretical foundation for workable organization policy will not automatically produce its implementation in practice. As NASA has found, numerous obstacles to organizational change can appear. For example, structural redesign may have little immediate impact on employee motivation; despite reforms, the space agency continues to suffer from poor internal morale and a general "malaise" (Matlack, 18 July 1987, p. 1857). Similarly, environmental factors may be difficult, if not impossible, to manipulate. Key Reagan staffers remained inexorably opposed to NASA's efforts to keep humans in space, while the general public is steadfastly indifferent. Finally, much like elephants, organizations are notoriously hard to budge; inertia can be considerable. Despite the glare of publicity and the harsh criticism that followed the *Challenger* explosion, NASA's procedures seem to have changed remarkably little. The agency kept the solid rocket booster used by the shuttle, merely adding a third O-ring and heating devices to warm the O-rings. That a completely new design might be needed evidently was not considered (Matlack, 11 April 1987); nor is there an "adequate backup design" in case the booster fails again (Matlack, 18 July 1987, p. 1850). Thus, both short- and long-run considerations militate against rapid change following organizational redesign.

Change is especially likely to be slow, of course, when the proposed change is based upon theoretical speculations, and even more so when those speculations run against the conventional wisdom. It hardly needs to be reiterated that our analysis and suggested prescriptions flow from a theoretical logic that is essentially untested empirically. Our descriptions of organizational governance are largely examples and anecdotes rather than the product of an exhaustive survey. We can offer logical arguments about structural congruence, and indeed doing so is a necessary first step. But real confidence in any theory requires systematic testing.

Nevertheless, it is clear that public organizations are, in a significant sense, polities. It follows that as an informal tool the governance model can aid us even now in recognizing and responding to a set of organizational realities that have received too little attention in the past. While we may be far from true organization policy—and, indeed, humans may be doomed to failure—we nonetheless can benefit from a capacity to see organizations in more of their dimensions. The possible fruits of such a quest justify its pursuit: enhanced governmental performance, heightened legitimacy, and more meaningful citizenship for the hundreds of thousands who labor in public organizations. We may never fully understand the organizational elephant, but as long as we cannot avoid the task of herding the beasts, the more we know, the better.

Bibliography

Aaron, Henry. *Politics and the Professors.* Washington, D.C.: Brookings Institution, 1978.

Aberbach, Joel D., and Bert A. Rockman. "Clashing Beliefs within the Executive Branch: The Nixon Administration Bureaucracy." *American Political Science Review* 70 (June 1976): 456–68.

Aberbach, Joel, and Bert Rockman. "Mandates or Mandarins? Control and Discretion in the Modern Administrative State." Paper presented at the annual meeting of the Western Political Science Association, Anaheim, Calif., 1987.

Abrahamsson, Bengt. *Bureaucracy or Participation: The Logic of Organization.* Beverly Hills, Calif.: Sage, 1977.

Abrams, Nancy Ellen, and R. Stephen Berry. "Mediation: A Better Alternative to Science Courts." *Bulletin of the Atomic Scientists* (April 1977): 50–53.

Allen, Robert W., Dan L. Madison, Lyman W. Porter, Patricia Renwick, and Bronston T. Mayes. "Organizational Politics: Tactics and Characteristics of Its Actors." *California Management Review* 22 (1979): 77–83.

Allen, Robert W., and Lyman W. Porter, editors. *Organizational Influence Processes.* Glenview, Ill.: Scott, Foresman, 1983.

Allison, Graham T. *Essence of Decision.* Boston: Little, Brown, 1971.

Appleby, Paul H. *Policy and Administration.* University, Ala.: University of Alabama Press, 1949.

Arrow, Kenneth J. *The Limits of Organization.* New York: Norton, 1974.

Bacharach, Samuel B., and Edward J. Lawler. *Power and Politics in Organizations.* San Francisco: Jossey-Bass, 1980.

Bacow, Lawrence S., and Michael Wheeler. *Environmental Dispute Resolution.* New York: Plenum, 1984.

Baldwin, Fred D. *Conflicting Interests: Corporate Governance Controversies.* Lexington, Mass.: Lexington Books, 1983.

Balutis, Alan P. "Improving Governmental Management Systems." In *Performance and Credibility: Developing Excellence in Public and Nonprofit Organizations,* edited by Joseph S. Wholey, Mark A. Abramson, and Christopher Bellavita. Lexington, Mass.: D. C. Heath, 1986, pp. 207–20.

Barber, Benjamin. *Strong Democracy: Participatory Politics for a New Age.* Berkeley: University of California Press, 1984.

Barber, William J. *From New Era to New Deal: Herbert Hoover, the Economists, and American Policy, 1921–1933.* Cambridge: Cambridge University Press, 1985.

Bell, Robert. "Professional Values and Organizational Decision Making." *Administration and Society* 17 (May 1985): 21–60.

Bellah, Robert N., Richard Madsen, William M. Sullivan, Ann Swidler, and Steven M. Tipton. *Habits of the Heart: Individualism and Commitment in American Life.* Berkeley: University of California Press, 1985.

Bendor, Jonathan B. *Parallel Systems: Redundancy in Government.* Berkeley: University of California Press, 1985.

Bendor, Jonathan, Serge Taylor, and Rolan Van Gaalen. "Stacking the Deck: Bureaucratic Missions and Policy Design." *American Political Science Review* 81 (September 1987): 873–96.

Benjamin, Roger W., and Stephen L. Elkin, editors. *The Democratic State.* Lawrence, Kans.: University Press of Kansas, 1985.

Benveniste, Guy. *Professionalizing the Organization: Reducing Bureaucracy to Enhance Effectiveness.* San Francisco: Jossey-Bass, 1987.

Bernstein, Harry. "Teachers' Role in Management May Improve LA Schools." *Los Angeles Times,* 22 March 1988, pp. 1, 19.

Blau, Peter M. "A Formal Theory of Differentiation in Organizations." *American Sociological Review* 35 (April 1970): 201–18.

Blau, Peter M., and Richard A. Schoenherr. *The Structure of Organizations.* New York: Basic Books, 1971.

Bolman, Lee G., and Terrence E. Deal. *Modern Approaches to Understanding and Managing Organizations.* San Francisco: Jossey-Bass, 1984.

Boschken, Herman L., and Susan L. Shumaker. "Public Agencies in Transition: A Strategic Management Approach in Pacific Coast Port Authorities." Paper presented at the annual meeting of the Midwest Political Science Association, Chicago, 1987.

Bozeman, Barry. *All Organizations Are Public: Bridging Public and Private Organizational Theories.* San Francisco: Jossey-Bass, 1987.

Bragaw, Louis K. *Managing a Federal Agency: The Hidden Stimulus.* Baltimore: Johns Hopkins University Press, 1980.

Braybrooke, David, and Charles E. Lindblom. *A Strategy of Decision: Policy Evaluation as a Social Process.* New York: Free Press, 1963.

Brett, Jeanne M., and Stephen B. Goldberg. "Mediator-Advisers: A New Third Party Role." In *Negotiating in Organizations,* edited by Max H. Bazerman and Roy J. Lewicki. Beverly Hills, Calif.: Sage, 1983, pp. 165-76.

Brintnall, Michael. "Organizational Change and Policy Change at the Department of Housing and Urban Development." Paper presented at the annual meeting of the American Political Science Association, Washington, D.C., 1986.

Browne, Angela, and Aaron Wildavsky. "Implementation as Exploration." In *Implementation: How Great Expectations in Washington Are Dashed in Oakland,* edited by Jeffrey L. Pressman and Aaron Wildavsky. 3d ed. Berkeley: University of California Press, 1984, pp. 232–56.

Bryner, Gary. "Assessing Environmental and Health Risks in Regulatory Agencies." Paper presented at the annual meeting of the Midwest Political Science Association, Chicago, 1986.

Bryner, Gary C. *Bureaucratic Discretion: Law and Policy in Federal Regulatory Agencies.* New York: Pergamon Press, 1987.

Bryson, John M. "The Policy Process and Organizational Form." *Policy Studies Journal* 12 (March 1984): 445–63.

Burford, Anne M., with John Greenya. *Are You Tough Enough? An Insider's View of Washington Power Politics.* New York: McGraw-Hill, 1986.

Burke, John P. *Bureaucratic Responsibility.* Baltimore: Johns Hopkins University Press, 1986.

Burns, James MacGregor. *Leadership.* New York: Harper & Row, 1978.

Burns, Tom, and G. M. Stalker. *The Management of Innovation.* London: Tavistock, 1961.

Cameron, Kim S., Myung U. Kim, and David A. Whetten. "Organizational Effects of Decline and Turbulence." *Administrative Science Quarterly* 32 (June 1987): 222–40.

Campbell, Colin, S.J. *Managing the Presidency: Carter, Reagan, and the Search for Executive Harmony.* Pittsburgh: University of Pittsburgh Press, 1986.

Chamberlin, John R., and John E. Jackson. "Privatization as Institutional Choice." *Journal of Policy Analysis and Management* 6 (Summer 1987): 586–604.

Chubb, John E. "Why the Current Wave of School Reform Will Fail." *The Public Interest* no. 90 (Winter 1988): 28–49.

Clingermayer, James C. "Government-Sponsored Consumer Advocacy and the Cost of Capital: The Case of Electric Utility Rate Regulation." Paper presented at the annual meeting of the Southern Political Science Association, Atlanta, 1986.

Cohen, Michael D., James G. March, and Johan P. Olsen. "People, Problems, Solutions, and the Ambiguity of Relevance." In *Ambiguity and Choice in Organizations,* edited by James G. March and Johan P. Olsen. Bergen, Norway: Universitetsforlaget, 1976, pp. 24–37.

Cole, Leonard. "Scientific Knowledge and Political Confusion." Paper presented at the annual meeting of the American Political Science Association, Chicago, 1987.

Cole, Richard L., and David A. Caputo. "Presidential Control of the Senior Civil Service: Assessing the Strategies of the Nixon Years." *American Political Science Review* 73 (June 1979): 399–413.

Connolly, Terry, Edward J. Conlon, and Stuart Jay Deutsch. "Organizational Effectiveness: A Multi Constituency Approach." *Academy of Management Review* 5 (April 1980): 211–17.

Cotton, John L., David A. Vollrath, Kirk L. Frogatt, Mark L. Lengnick-Hall, and Kenneth R. Jennings. "Employee Participation: Diverse Forms and Different Outcomes." *Academy of Management Review* 13 (Winter 1988): 8–22.

Cox, Raymond W., and Michael R. King. "American State Legislatures: Models of Organization and Reform." Paper presented at the annual meeting of the Midwest Political Science Association, Chicago, 1985.

Crandall, Robert W., and Lester B. Lave. *The Scientific Basis of Health and Safety Regulation.* Washington, D.C.: Brookings Institution, 1981.

Crozier, Michel. *The Bureaucratic Phenomenon.* Chicago: University of Chicago Press, 1964.

Cyert, Richard, and James March. *A Behavioral Theory of the Firm.* Englewood Cliffs, N.J.: Prentice-Hall, 1963.

Dahl, Robert. *Polyarchy: Participation and Opposition.* New Haven: Yale University Press, 1971.

Dahl, Robert A., and Charles E. Lindblom. *Politics, Economics and Welfare.* New York: Harper, 1953.

Davidson, Roger, and Walter J. Oleszek. "Adaptation and Consolidation: Structural Innovation in the U.S. House of Representatives." *Legislative Studies Quarterly* 1 (February 1976): 37–65.

Delbecq, Andre, Andrew Van de Ven, and David Gustavson. *Group Techniques for Program Planning.* Glenview, Ill.: Scott, Foresman, 1975.

Denhardt, Kathryn G. "Organizational Dimensions of Administrative Ethics." Paper presented at the annual meeting of the Southern Political Science Association, Charlotte, North Carolina, 1987.

Denhardt, Robert B. *Theories of Public Organizations.* Pacific Grove, Calif.: Brooks/Cole, 1984.

Denhardt, Robert B., James Pyle, and Allen C. Bluedorn. "Implementing Quality Circles in State Government." *Public Administration Review* 47 (July/August 1987): 304–09.

Dery, David. *Problem Definition in Policy Analysis.* Lawrence, Kans.: University Press of Kansas, 1984.

Diamant, Alfred. "Workplace Democracy: Some Thoughts on Organizational Culture." Paper presented at the annual meeting of the Midwest Political Science Association, Chicago, 1986.

DiMaggio, Paul J., and Walter W. Powell. "The Iron Cage Revisited: Institutional Isomorphism and Collective Rationality in Organizational Fields." *American Sociological Review* 48 (April 1983): 147–60.

Diver, Colin S. "Policy Making Paradigms in Administrative Law." *Harvard Law Review* 95 (December 1981): 363–434.

Douglas, Mary, and Aaron Wildavsky. *Risk and Culture.* Berkeley: University of California Press, 1982.

Dow, Gregory K. "Configurational and Coactivational Views of Organizational Structure." *Academy of Management Review* 13 (Winter 1988): 53–64.

Downey, Gary L. "Federalism and Nuclear Waste Disposal: The Struggle over Shared Decision Making." *Journal of Policy Analysis and Management* 5 (Fall 1985): 73–99.

Downs, Anthony. *Inside Bureaucracy.* New York: Little, Brown, 1967.

Dror, Yehezkel. *Policymaking under Adversity.* New Brunswick, N.J.: Transaction Books, 1986.

Dye, Lee. "Improved Shuttle to Resurrect America's Adventure in Space." *Los Angeles Times,* 19 June 1988, pp. 3, 30, 32.

Easterbrook, Frank H. "An Immutable Vision." *Washington Post Magazine* 28 (June 1987): 52–56.

Eisenberg, Melvin Aron. "Participation, Responsiveness, and the Consultative Process: An Essay for Lon Fuller." *Harvard Law Review* 92 (December 1978): 410–32.

Etzioni, Amitai. *A Comparative Analysis of Complex Organizations.* Rev. ed. New York: Free Press, 1975.

Eulau, Heinz. *Politics, Self, and Society: A Theme and Variations.* Cambridge, Mass.: Harvard University Press, 1986.

Evan, William M. "Power, Conflict, and Constitutionalism in Organizations." In *Organization Theory: Structures, Systems, and Environments,* edited by William M. Evan. New York: Wiley, 1976, pp. 83–111.

Ferguson, Kathy. *The Feminist Case against Bureaucracy.* Philadelphia: Temple University Press, 1984.

Ferris, James M. "Coprovision: Citizen Time and Money Donations in Public Service Provision." *Public Administration Review* 44 (July/August 1984): 324–33.

Finer, Herman. "Administrative Responsibility in Democratic Government." *Public Administration Review* 1 (1941): 335–50.

Fiorino, Daniel J. "Regulatory Negotiation as a Policy Process." *Public Administration Review* 48 (July/August 1988): 764–72.

Frederickson, James W. "Strategic Decision Process and Organizational Structure." *Academy of Management Review* 11 (April 1986): 280–97.

Friedman, Robert S. "Using Consultation and Compensation in Siting Repositories for High-Level Nuclear Waste." *Journal of Policy Analysis and Management* 17 (Fall 1987): 141–45.

Friedrich, Carl Joachim. "Public Policy and the Nature of Administrative Responsibility." *Public Policy* 1 (1940): 3–24.

Fritschler, A. Lee. *Smoking and Politics: Policymaking and the Federal Bureaucracy.* 3d ed. Englewood Cliffs, N.J.: Prentice-Hall, 1983.

Fuller, Lon. "The Forms and Limits of Adjudication." *Harvard Law Review* 92 (December 1978): 353–409.

Gage, Robert W. "Federal Regional Councils: Networking Organizations for Policy Management." *Public Administration Review* 44 (March/April 1984): 134–45.

Galaskiewicz, Joseph. *Exchange Networks and Community Politics.* Beverly Hills, Calif.: Sage, 1979.

Gawthrop, Louis C. *Public Sector Management, Systems, and Ethics.* Bloomington, Ind.: Indiana University Press, 1984.

Gormley, William T., Jr. "Muscles and Prayers: Bureau Busting in the 1970s." Paper presented at the annual meeting of the American Political Science Association, Washington, D.C., 1986. (a)

Gormley, William T., Jr. "The Representation Revolution: Reforming State Regulation through Public Representation." *Administration and Society* 18 (August 1986): 179–96. (b)

Gormley, William T., Jr. "Institutional Policy Analysis: A Critical Review." *Journal of Policy Analysis and Management* 6 (Winter 1987): 153–69.

Gormley, William T., Jr., and B. Guy Peters. "Policy Problems and Their Remedies." Paper presented at the annual meeting of the Midwest Political Science Association, Chicago, 1987.

Gortner, Harold F., Julianne Mahler, and Jeanne Bell Nicholson. *Organization Theory: A Public Perspective.* Chicago: Dorsey, 1987.

Gray, Barbara, and Sonny S. Ariss. "Political and Strategic Change Across Organizational Life Cycles." *Academy of Management Review* 10 (October 1985): 707–23.

Green, Philip. *Retrieving Democracy: In Search of Civic Equality.* Totawa, N.J.: Rowman and Allanheld, 1985.

Greenwood, Ted. *Knowledge and Discretion in Government Regulation.* New York: Praeger, 1984.

Gruber, Judith E. *Controlling Bureaucracies: Dilemmas in Democratic Governance.* Berkeley: University of California Press, 1987.

Gulick, Luther, and L. Urwick. *Papers on the Science of Administration.* New York: Institute of Public Administration, Columbia University, 1937.

Hage, Jerald. *Theories of Organizations: Form, Process, and Transformation.* New York: Wiley, 1980.

Hale, Dennis. "Just What Is Policy Anyway and Who's Supposed to Make It? A Survey of the Public Administration and Policy Texts." *Administration and Society* 19 (February 1988): 423–52.

Hall, Richard H. *Organizations: Structures, Processes, and Outcomes.* 4th ed. Englewood Cliffs, N.J.: Prentice-Hall, 1987.

Halperin, Morton H., with the assistance of Priscilla Clapp and Arnold Kanter. *Bureaucratic Politics and Foreign Policy.* Washington, D.C.: Brookings Institution, 1974.

Hammond, Thomas. "Agenda Control, Organizational Structure, and Bureaucratic Politics." *American Journal of Political Science* 30 (May 1986): 379–420.

Hammond, Thomas, and Gary J. Miller. "A Social Choice Perspective on Expertise and Authority in Bureaucracy." *American Journal of Political Science* 29 (February 1985): 1–28.

Hanf, Kenneth. "Introduction." In *Interorganizational Policy Making: Limits to Coordination and Central Control,* edited by Kenneth Hanf and Fritz W. Scharpf. Beverly Hills, Calif.: Sage, 1978, pp. 1–15.

Hannan, Michael T., and John H. Freeman. "Internal Politics of Growth and Decline." In *Environment and Organizations,* edited by Marshall Meyer and associates. San Francisco: Jossey-Bass, 1977, pp. 131–71. (a)

Hannan, Michael T., and John H. Freeman. "The Population Ecology Model of Organizations." *American Journal of Sociology* 82 (March 1977): 929–64. (b)

Harmon, Michael M. *Action Theory for Public Administration.* New York: Longman, 1981.

Harmon, Michael M., and Richard T. Mayer. *Organization Theory for Public Administration.* Boston: Little, Brown, 1986.

Hattis, Dale, and David Kennedy. "Assessing Risks from Health Hazards: An Imperfect Science." *Technology Review* (May/June 1986): 60–71.

Heclo, Hugh. *A Government of Strangers.* Washington, D.C.: Brookings Institution, 1977.

Heclo, Hugh. "Issue Networks and the Executive Establishment." In *The New American Political System,* edited by Anthony King. Washington, D.C.: American Enterprise Institute, 1978, pp. 87–124.

Hess, Stephen. *Organizing the Presidency.* Washington, D.C.: Brookings Institution, 1976.

Heymann, Philip B. *The Politics of Public Management.* New Haven: Yale University Press, 1987.

Hoel, David G., and Kenny S. Crump. "Waterborne Carcinogens: A Scientist's View." In *The Scientific Basis of Health and Safety Regulation,* edited by Robert W. Crandall and Lester B. Lave. Washington, D.C.: Brookings Institution, 1981, pp. 173–95.

Holden, Matthew. " 'Imperialism' in Bureaucracy." *American Political Science Review* 60 (December 1966): 943–51.

Holzer, Marc. "Productivity in, Garbage out: Sanitation Gains in New York." *Public Productivity Review* 11 (Spring 1988): 37–50.

Hood, Christopher C. *The Limits of Administration.* New York: Wiley, 1976.

Hood, Christopher C. *Administrative Analysis: An Introduction to Rules, Enforcement, and Organizations.* New York: St. Martin's, 1986.

Hoover, Kenneth R. *Ideology and Political Life.* Pacific Grove, Calif.: Brooks/Cole, 1987.

Hoover, Kenneth R. *The Elements of Social Scientific Thinking.* 4th ed. New York: St. Martin's, 1988.

Horowitz, Donald. *The Courts and Social Policy.* Washington, D.C.: Brookings Institution, 1977.

Hult, Karen M. *Agency Merger and Bureaucratic Redesign.* Pittsburgh: University of Pittsburgh Press, 1987.

Hult, Karen M. "Governing in Bureaucracies: The Case of Parental Notification." *Administration and Society* 20 (November 1988): 313–33.

Ingraham, Patricia A. "Toward More Systematic Consideration of Policy Design." *Policy Studies Journal* 15 (June 1987): 611–28.

Janis, Irving. *Victims of Groupthink.* Boston: Houghton Mifflin, 1972.

Janowitz, Morris. "Observations on the Sociology of Citizenship: Obligations and Rights." *Social Forces* 59 (September 1980): 1–24.

Jordan, A. Grant. "Iron Triangles, Woolly Corporatism, and Elastic Nets: Images of the Policy Process." *Journal of Public Policy* 1 (February 1981): 95–123.

Jowell, Jeffrey L. *Law and Bureaucracy: Administrative Discretion and the Limits of Legal Action.* Port Washington, N.Y.: Dunellen, 1975.

Kamlet, Mark S., David C. Mowery, and Tsai-Tsu Su. "Who Do You Trust? An Analysis of Executive and Congressional Economic Forecasts." Paper presented at the annual meeting of the Midwest Political Science Association, Chicago, 1986.

Kanter, Rosabeth Moss. *Men and Women of the Corporation.* New York: Basic Books, 1977.

Kanter, Rosabeth Moss. *The Change Masters.* New York: Simon and Schuster, 1983.

Kantrowitz, Arthur. "The Science Court Experiment: Criticisms and Responses." *Bulletin of the Atomic Scientists* (April 1977): 45–50.

Kaplan, Abraham. *The Conduct of Inquiry: Methodology for Behavioral Science.* New York: Harper & Row, 1963.

Katz, Daniel. "The Motivational Bases for Organizational Behavior." *Behavioral Science* 9 (April 1964): 131–46.

Katz, Daniel, and Robert L. Kahn. *The Social Psychology of Organizations.* 2d ed. New York: Wiley, 1978.

Kaufman, Herbert. *The Forest Ranger.* Baltimore: Johns Hopkins University Press, 1960.

Kaufman, Herbert. "Organization Theory and Political Theory." *American Political Science Review* 58 (March 1964): 5–14.

Kaufman, Herbert. *Are Government Organizations Immortal?* Washington, D.C.: Brookings Institution, 1976.

Kaufman, Herbert. *The Administrative Behavior of Federal Bureau Chiefs.* Washington, D.C.: Brookings Institution, 1981.

Kaufman, Herbert. *Time, Chance, and Organizations: Natural Selection in a Perilous Environment.* Chatham, N.J.: Chatham House, 1985.

Kernell, Samuel, and Samuel Popkin, editors. *Chief of Staff: Twenty-Five Years of Managing the Presidency.* Berkeley: University of California Press, 1986.

Kettl, Donald F. *Government by Proxy: (Mis?)Managing Federal Programs.* Washington, D.C.: Congressional Quarterly, 1988.

Khandwalla, Pradip N. *The Design of Organizations.* New York: Harcourt Brace Jovanovich, 1977.

Kimm, Victor J., Arnold M. Kuzmack, and David W. Schnare. "Waterborne Carcinogens: A Regulator's View." In *The Scientific Basis of Health and Safety Regulation,* edited by Robert W. Crandall and Lester B. Lave. Washington, D.C.: Brookings Institution, 1981, pp. 229–49.

Kirschten, Dick. "Competent Manager." *National Journal,* 28 February 1987, pp. 468–79. (a)

Kirschten, Dick. "White House Notebook." *National Journal,* 4 April 1987, 23 May 1987, 1 August 1987. (b)

Knott, Jack H., and Gary Miller. "Dilemmas in Teams and Firms: Experiments on Simple Hierarchies." Paper presented at the annual meeting of the American Political Science Association, Washington, D.C., 1986.

Knott, Jack H., and Gary J. Miller. *Reforming Bureaucracy: The Politics of Institutional Choice.* Englewood Cliffs, N.J.: Prentice-Hall, 1987.

Kraft, Michael E., and Norman J. Vig. "Environmental Policy Change in the Reagan Presidency." Paper presented at the annual meeting of the American Political Science Association, Chicago, 1983.

Kraus, William A. *Collaboration in Organizations: Alternatives to Hierarchy.* New York: Human Sciences Press, 1980.

Krepon, Michael. "CIA, DIA at Odds over Soviet Threat." *Bulletin of the Atomic Scientists* 43 (May 1987): 6–7.

Kriz, Margaret E. "Kibitzer with Clout." *National Journal,* 30 May 1987, pp. 1404–08.

Landau, Madeline. *Race, Poverty and the Cities: Hyperinnovation in Complex Policy Systems.* Berkeley: Institute of Policy Studies, University of California, 1988.

Landau, Martin. "Redundancy, Rationality, and the Problem of Duplication and Overlap." *Public Administration Review* 29 (1969): 346–58.

Landau, Martin. *Political Theory and Political Science.* New York: Macmillan, 1972.

Landau, Martin. "On the Concept of a Self-Correcting Organization." *Public Administration Review* 33 (November/December 1973): 533–42.

Landau, Martin. Phi Beta Kappa Lecture. Hamline University, December 1983.

Landau, Martin, and Russell Stout. "To Manage Is Not to Control, or the Folly of Type II Errors." *Public Administration Review* 39 (March/April 1979): 148–56.

Lange, Elaine. "Prison, Poison, Uncertainty Absorption: Routinizing Decision-making When Experts Disagree." In *JAI 1988 Research Annual in*

Public Policy Analysis and Management, edited by Stuart S. Nagel. Greenwich, Conn.: JAI Press, 1988, pp. 103–33.

LaPorte, Todd R. "Complexity and Uncertainty: Challenge to Action." In *Organized Social Complexity: Challenge to Politics and Policy,* edited by Todd R. LaPorte. Princeton, N.J.: Princeton University Press, 1975, pp. 332–56.

Laumann, Edward O. *Networks of Collective Action.* New York: Academic Press, 1976.

Laumann, Edward O., Joseph Galaskiewicz, and Peter V. Marsden. "Community Structure as Interorganizational Linkage." *Annual Review of Sociology* 4 (1978): 455–84.

Lawler, Edward E., III. *High-Involvement Management: Participative Strategies for Improving Organizational Performance.* San Francisco: Jossey-Bass, 1986.

Lawler, James J., and William Parle. "Risk Communication and the NIMBY Syndrome in Hazardous Waste Decision-making: Reconciling Technical Opinion and Citizen Participation." Paper presented at the annual meeting of the Western Political Science Association, San Francisco, 1988.

Lawrence, P. R., and J. W. Lorsch. *Organization and Environment.* Cambridge, Mass.: Harvard Graduate School of Business Administration, 1967.

Lewis, Eugene. *Public Entrepreneurship: Toward a Theory of Bureaucratic Political Power.* Bloomington, Ind.: Indiana University Press, 1980.

Lindblom, Charles. "The Science of Muddling Through." *Public Administration Review* 19 (Spring 1959): 79–88.

Linder, Stephen H., and B. Guy Peters. "A Design Perspective on Policy Implementation: The Fallacies of Misplaced Prescription." *Policy Studies Review* 6 (February 1987): 459–75.

Los Angeles Times. "Overruling of Engineers for the Shuttle Probed." 21 February 1986, pp. 1, 14.

Los Angeles Times. "Report to Blame NASA 'Baronies.' " 8 June 1986, pp. 1, 24–25.

Los Angeles Times. "Feynman Issues Report—More Critical than Panel's." 11 June 1986, pp. 1, 22.

Lowi, Theodore. *The End of Liberalism.* 2d ed. New York: Norton, 1979.

Lustick, Ian. "Explaining the Variable Utility of Disjointed Incrementalism: Four Propositions." *American Political Science Review* 74 (June 1980): 342–53.

Lynn, Laurence E., Jr. *Managing the Public's Business: The Job of the Government Executive.* New York: Basic Books, 1981.

Lynn, Laurence E., Jr. "The Reagan Administration and the Renitent Bureaucracy." In *The Reagan Presidency and the Governing of America,* edited by Lester M. Salamon and Michael S. Lund. Washington, D.C.: Urban Institute Press, 1984, pp. 339–70.

Maccoby, Michael. *The Gamesman.* New York: Simon and Schuster, 1976.

Mackenzie, Kenneth D. *Organizational Design: The Organizational Audit and Analysis Technology.* Norwood, N.J.: Ablex Publishing, 1986.

Mahler, Julianne G. "Structured Decision Making in Public Organizations." *Public Administration Review* 47 (July/August 1987): 336–42.

Mansbridge, Jane J. *Beyond Adversarial Democracy.* New York: Basic Books, 1980.

March, James G. "The Business Firm as a Political Coalition." *Journal of Politics* 24 (November 1962): 662–78.

March, James G., and Johan P. Olsen. "Organizing for Political Life: What Administrative Reorganization Tells Us about Government." *American Political Science Review* 77 (June 1983): 281–96.

March, James G., and Johan P. Olsen. "The New Institutionalism: Organizational Factors in Political Life." *American Political Science Review* 78 (September 1984): 734–49.

March, James G., and Herbert Simon. *Organizations.* New York: Wiley, 1958.

Marini, Frank, editor. *Toward a New Public Administration: The Minnowbrook Perspective.* Scranton, Pa.: Chandler Publishing, 1971.

Martin, Jeffrey N. "Note: Procedures for Decisionmaking under Conditions of Scientific Uncertainty: The Science Court Proposal." *Harvard Journal on Legislation* 16 (Spring 1979): 443–511.

Mashaw, Jerry L. *Bureaucratic Justice: Managing Social Security Disability Claims.* New Haven: Yale University Press, 1983.

Mashaw, Jerry L. *Due Process in the Administrative State.* New Haven: Yale University Press, 1985.

Mason, Ronald M. *Participatory and Workplace Democracy: A Theoretical Development in Critique of Liberalism.* Carbondale, Ill.: Southern Illinois University Press, 1982.

Matlack, Carol. "Betting on Safety." *National Journal,* 11 April 1987, p. 911.

Matlack, Carol. "NASA Still Waiting for a Liftoff." *National Journal* 18 (July 1987): 1850.

Mayes, Bronston T., and Robert W. Allen. "Toward a Definition of Organizational Politics." *Academy of Management Review* 2 (October 1977): 672–78.

Maynard-Moody, Steven, Michael Musheno, Dennis Palumbo, and Annamarie Oliverio. "Street-wise Social Policy: Empowering Workers to Resolve the Dilemma of Discretion and Accountability." Paper presented at the annual meeting of the American Political Science Association, Chicago, 1987.

Maynard-Moody, Steven, Donald D. Stull, and Jerry Mitchell. "Reorganization as Status Drama: Building, Maintaining, and Displacing Dominant Subcultures." *Public Administration Review* 46 (July/August 1986): 301–10.

Mazmanian, Daniel. "Toxics Policy in California: New Directions in Environmental Policy Making." Unpublished manuscript, November 1987.

Mazmanian, Daniel A., and David Morrell. "Policy Escalation: The Elusive Pursuit of Toxics Management." *The Public Interest,* no. 90 (Winter 1988): 81–98.

Mazmanian, Daniel A., and Paul A. Sabatier. *Effective Policy Implementation.* Lexington, Mass.: D. C. Heath, 1981.

McCabe, Amy Snyder, and Michael R. Fitzgerald. "Open Systems of Environmental Decision-making: The MRS Nuclear Waste Siting Case in Tennessee." Paper presented at the annual meeting of the American Political Science Association, Chicago, 1987.

McGarity, Thomas O. "Substantive and Procedural Discretion in Administrative Resolution of Science Policy Questions: Regulating Carcinogens in EPA and OSHA." *Georgetown Law Journal* 67 (February 1979): 729–810.

Mead, Lawrence M. *Beyond Entitlement: The Social Obligations of Citizenship.* New York: Free Press, 1986.

Meier, Kenneth J. "Executive Reorganization of Government: Impact on Employment and Expenditures." *American Journal of Political Science* 24 (August 1980): 386–412.

Melnick, R. Shep. *Regulation and the Courts: The Case of the Clean Air Act.* Washington, D.C.: Brookings Institution, 1983.

Meltsner, Arnold J., and Christopher Bellavita. *The Policy Organization.* Beverly Hills, Calif.: Sage, 1983.

Merkle, Judith A. *Management and Ideology: The Legacy of the International Scientific Management Movement.* Berkeley: University of California Press, 1980.

Merton, Robert K. "Bureaucratic Structure and Personality." *Social Forces* 18 (May 1940): 560–68.

Meyer, John, and Brian Rowan. "Institutionalized Organizations: Formal Structure as Myth and Ceremony." *American Journal of Sociology* 83 (September 1977): 340–63.

Meyer, Marshall W. *Change in Public Bureaucracies.* Cambridge: Cambridge University Press, 1979.

Meyer, Marshall W., and associates, editors. *Environment and Organizations: Theoretical and Empirical Perspectives.* San Francisco: Jossey-Bass, 1978.

Miller, Gary J., and Terry M. Moe. "The Positive Theory of Hierarchies." Paper presented at the annual meeting of the American Political Science Association, Chicago, 1983.

Mintzberg, Henry. *The Structure of Organizations.* Englewood Cliffs, N.J.: Prentice-Hall, 1982.

Mintzberg, Henry. *Power in and around Organizations.* Englewood Cliffs, N.J.: Prentice-Hall, 1983.

Mitchell, Terence R., and William G. Scott. "Leadership Failures, the Distrusting Public, and Prospects of the Administrative State." *Public Administration Review* 47 (November/December 1987): 445–52.

Moe, Terry. "The Politicized Presidency." In *The New Direction in American Politics*, edited by John E. Chubb and Paul E. Peterson. Washington, D.C.: Brookings Institution, 1985, pp. 235–72.

Moe, Terry. "Political Control and Professional Autonomy: The Institutional Politics of the NLRB." Paper presented at the annual meeting of the American Political Science Association, Washington, D.C., 1986.

Moore, Charles H., David W. Sink, and Patricia Hoban-Moore. "The Politics of Homelessness." *PS: Political Science and Politics* 21 (Winter 1988): 57–63.

Moore, Scott T. "The Place of Power in Organization Theory." Paper presented at the annual meeting of the American Political Science Association, Washington, D.C., 1986.

Morell, David. "Technological Policies and Hazardous Waste Politics in California." In *The Politics of Hazardous Waste Management*, edited by James Lester and Ann Bowman. Durham, N.C.: Duke University Press, 1983, pp. 139–75.

Morgan, Douglas F. "Varieties of Administrative Abuse: Some Reflections on Ethics and Discretion." *Administration and Society* 19 (November 1987): 267–84.

Morgan, Gareth. *Images of Organization*. Beverly Hills, Calif.: Sage, 1986.

Morse, C. Wesley. *Environmental Consultation*. New York: Praeger, 1984.

Mosher, Frederick C. *Democracy and the Public Service*. New York: Oxford University Press, 1968.

Nachmias, David, and Chava Nachmias. *Research Methods in the Social Sciences*. 3d ed. New York: St. Martin's Press, 1987.

Nadler, David A., and Michael L. Tushman. "A Model for Diagnosing Organizational Behavior." *Organizational Dynamics* (Autumn 1980): 35–51.

Nagel, Jack H. *Participation*. Englewood Cliffs, N.J.: Prentice-Hall, 1987.

Nathan, Richard. *The Administrative Presidency*. New York: Wiley, 1983.

Nelkin, Dorothy. "Science, Technology, and Political Conflict: Analyzing the Issues." In *Controversy: Politics of Technical Decisions*, edited by Dorothy Nelkin. 2d ed. Beverly Hills, Calif.: Sage, 1984, pp. 9–24.

Nelkin, Dorothy, and Michael Pollak. "Problems and Procedures in the Regulation of Technological Risk." In *Making Bureaucracies Work*, edited by Carol H. Weiss and Allen H. Barton. Beverly Hills, Calif.: Sage, 1980, pp. 259–78.

Newman, Katherine. "Incipient Bureaucracy: The Development of Hierarchies in Egalitarian Organizations." In *Hierarchy and Society: An Anthropological Perspective on Bureaucracy*, edited by Gerald M. Britan and Ronald Cohen. Philadelphia: Institute for the Study of Human Issues, 1980, pp. 143–63.

New York Times. "For Former Head of NASA, a Trial by Error." 26 June 1987, p. 10.

Nurick, Aaron J. *Participation in Organizational Change: The TVA Experiment*. New York: Praeger, 1985.

Olsen, Johan P. *Organized Democracy: Political Institutions in a Welfare State: The Case of Norway.* Bergen, Norway: Universitetsforlaget, 1983.

Organ, Dennis W. *Organizational Citizenship Behavior: The Good Soldier Syndrome.* Lexington, Mass.: Lexington Books, 1988.

Ortony, Andrew, editor. *Metaphor and Thought.* Cambridge: Cambridge University Press, 1980.

O'Toole, James. *Vanguard Management: Redesigning the Corporate Future.* Garden City, N.Y.: Doubleday, 1985.

O'Toole, Lawrence J., and Robert S. Montjoy. "Interorganizational Policy Implementation: A Theoretical Perspective."*Public Administration Review* 44 (November/December 1984): 491–503.

Ouchi, William G. "Markets, Bureaucracies, and Clans." *Administrative Science Quarterly* 25 (March 1980): 129–41.

Ouchi, William G. *Theory Z: How American Business Can Meet the Japanese Challenge.* New York: Avon Books, 1981.

Ozawa, Connie P., and Lawrence Susskind. "Mediating Science-intensive Policy Disputes." *Journal of Policy Analysis and Management* 5 (Fall 1985): 23–39.

Page, Talbot, Robert Harris, and Judith Bruser. "Waterborne Carcinogens: An Economist's View." In *The Scientific Basis of Health and Safety Regulation,* edited by Robert W. Crandall and Lester B. Lave. Washington, D.C.: Brookings Institution, 1981, pp. 197–228.

Pasmore, William A. "Power and Participation: The Coming Shake-up in Organizational Power Structures." In *Executive Power,* edited by Suresh Srivastra. San Francisco: Jossey-Bass, 1986, pp. 239–56.

Patchen, Martin. "Labor-Management Consultation at TVA: Its Impact on Employees." In *Participative Management: Concepts, Theory, and Implementation,* edited by Ervin Williams. Atlanta: Georgia State University Press, 1976, pp. 151–72.

Pateman, Carole. *Participation and Democratic Theory.* Cambridge: Cambridge University Press, 1970.

Pateman, Carole. "A Contribution to the Political Theory of Organizational Democracy." *Administration and Society* 7 (May 1975): 5–26.

Pennock, J. Roland. *Democratic Political Theory.* Princeton, N.J.: Princeton University Press, 1979.

Percy, Stephen L. "Citizen Coproduction: Prospects for Improving Service Delivery." *Journal of Urban Affairs* 5 (Summer 1983): 203–10.

Perrow, Charles. *Normal Accidents: Living with High Risk Technologies.* New York: Basic Books, 1984.

Perrow, Charles. *Complex Organizations: A Critical Essay.* New York: Random House, 1986.

Perry, James L. "Strategies for Building Public Administration Theory." Paper presented at the annual meeting of the American Political Science Association, Chicago, 1987.

Peters, Thomas J., and Robert H. Waterman. *In Search of Excellence*. New York: Warner Books, 1982.

Pettigrew, Andrew M. *The Politics of Organizational Decision-making*. London: Tavistock, 1973.

Pfeffer, Jeffrey. *Power in Organizations*. Marshfield, Mass.: Pitman, 1981.

Pfeffer, Jeffrey, and Gerald Salancik. *The External Control of Organizations: A Resource Dependence Perspective*. New York: Harper & Row, 1978.

Piasecki, Bruce, and Jerry Gravander. "The Missing Links: Restructuring Hazardous-Waste Controls in America." *Technology Review* (October 1985): 43–52.

Pitkin, Hanna Fenichel. *The Concept of Representation*. Berkeley: University of California Press, 1967.

Planned Parenthood Federation of America, Inc., et al. v. Richard S. Schweiker; National Family Planning and Reproductive Health Association, Inc., et al. v. DHHS. 559 F.Supp. 658 (1983); 712 F.2d. 650 (1983).

Popper, Andrew F. "An Administrative Law Perspective on Consensual Decision-making." *Administrative Law Review* 35 (Summer 1983): 255–312.

Porter, Lyman W., Robert W. Allen, and Harold C. Angle. "The Politics of Upward Influence in Organizations." In *Organizational Influence Processes*, edited by R. Allen and L. Porter. Glenview, Ill.: Scott, Foresman, 1983, pp. 408–22.

Porter, Roger B. "Roger B. Porter on How the White House Works." *Brookings Review* (Fall 1985): 37–40.

Powell, Walter W. *Getting into Print: The Decision-making Process in Scholarly Publishing*. Chicago: University of Chicago Press, 1985.

Pranger, Robert J. *The Eclipse of Citizenship: Power and Participation in Contemporary Politics*. New York: Holt, Rinehart & Winston, 1968.

Quinn, Robert E., and Richard H. Hall. "Environments, Organizations, and Policymakers: Toward an Integrative Framework." In *Organization Theory and Public Policy*, edited by Richard H. Hall and Robert E. Quinn. Beverly Hills, Calif.: Sage, 1983, pp. 281–98.

Rainey, Hal G., and H. Brinton Milward. "Public Organizations: Policy Networks and Environments." In *Organization Theory and Public Policy*, edited by Richard H. Hall and Robert E. Quinn. Beverly Hills, Calif.: Sage, 1983, pp. 133–46.

Ranney, Austin. " 'The Divine Science': Political Engineering in American Culture." *American Political Science Review* 70 (March 1976): 140–48.

Rather, Dan, and Gary Paul Gates. *The Palace Guard*. New York: Harper & Row, 1974.

Redford, Emmette S. *Democracy in the Administrative State*. New York: Oxford University Press, 1969.

"Rethinking Regulation: Negotiation as an Alternative to Traditional Rulemaking." *Harvard Law Review* 94 (June 1981): 1871–91.

Rhodes, Susan L. "Political Conflict and Technological Uncertainty in Bureaucratic Policy Making: Food and Drug Administration Regulation of Intrauterine Devices." Paper presented at the annual meeting of the Midwest Political Science Association, Milwaukee, 1982.

Rich, Richard C. "Interaction of Voluntary and Governmental Sectors: Toward an Understanding of the Coproduction of Municipal Services." *Administration and Society* 13 (May 1981): 59–76.

Riley, Dennis D. *Controlling the Federal Bureaucracy.* Philadelphia: Temple University Press, 1987.

Ripley, Randall B., and Grace A. Franklin. *Congress, the Bureaucracy, and Public Policy.* Homewood, Ill.: Dorsey, 1984.

Rittel, Horst W. J., and Melvin M. Webber. "Dilemmas in a General Theory of Planning." *Policy Sciences* 4 (June 1973): 155–69.

Roelofs, H. Mark. *The Tension of Citizenship: Private Man and Public Duty.* New York: Rinehart, 1957.

Romzek, Barbara S., and Melvin J. Dubnick. "Accountability in the Public Sector: Lessons from the *Challenger* Disaster." *Public Administration Review* 47 (May/June 1987): 227–38.

Rothschild, Joyce, and J. Allen Whitt. *The Cooperative Workplace: Potentials and Dilemmas of Organizational Democracy and Participation.* Cambridge: Cambridge University Press, 1986.

Rothschild-Whitt, Joyce. "The Collectivist Organization: An Alternative to Rational-Bureaucratic Models."*American Sociological Review* 44 (August 1979): 509–27.

Rourke, Francis E. *Bureaucracy, Politics, and Public Policy.* 3d ed. Boston: Little, Brown, 1984.

Sabatier, Paul. "The Acquisition and Utilization of Technical Information by Administrative Agencies." *Administrative Science Quarterly* 23 (September 1978): 396–417.

Sabatier, Paul. "Knowledge, Policy-oriented Learning, and Policy Change: An Advocacy Coalition Framework." *Knowledge: Creation, Diffusion, Utilization* 8 (1987): 649–92.

Sabatier, Paul A., and Neil Pelkey. "Incorporating Multiple Actors and Guidance Instruments into Models of Regulatory Policymaking: An Advocacy Coalition Framework." *Administration and Society* 19 (August 1987): 236–63.

Salamon, Lester M. "The Goals of Reorganization: A Framework for Analysis." *Administration and Society* 12 (February 1981): 471–500.

Sapolsky, Harvey M. *The Polaris System Development: Bureaucratic and Programmatic Success in Government.* Cambridge, Mass.: Harvard University Press, 1972.

Sapolsky, Harvey M. "A Solution to the 'Health Crisis.' " *Policy Analysis* 3 (Winter 1977): 115–21.

Saxe, John Godfrey. *Poetical Works.* Boston: Houghton Mifflin, 1882.

Schein, Edward H. *Organizational Culture*. San Francisco: Jossey-Bass, 1985.

Schiesl, Martin J. *The Politics of Efficiency: Municipal Administration and Reform in America, 1880–1920*. Berkeley: University of California Press, 1977.

Scholz, John. "Reliability, Responsiveness, and Regulatory Policy." *Public Administration Review* 44 (March/April 1984): 145–53.

Schon, Donald. "Generative Metaphor: A Perspective on Problem Setting in Social Policy." In *Metaphor and Thought*, edited by Andrew Ortony. Cambridge: Cambridge University Press, 1980, pp. 254–83.

Schuck, Peter H. "Litigation, Bargaining, and Regulation." *Regulation* 3 (July/August 1979): 26–34.

Schweiger, David M., William R. Sandberg, and James W. Ragan. "Group Approaches for Improving Strategic Decision Making: A Comparative Analysis of Dialectical Inquiry, Devil's Advocacy, and Consensus." *Academy of Management Journal* 29 (March 1986): 51–71.

Scott, William G. "Organization Government: The Prospects for a Truly Participative System." *Public Administration Review* 29 (January/February 1969): 43–53.

Seidman, Harold, and Robert Gilmour. *Politics, Position, and Power*. 4th ed. New York: Oxford University Press, 1986.

Shafritz, Jay M. *The Dorsey Dictionary of American Government and Politics*. Chicago: Dorsey, 1988.

Shafritz, Jay M., and J. Steven Ott. *Classics of Organization Theory*. 2d ed. Chicago: Dorsey, 1987.

Sheppard, Blair H. "Managers as Inquisitors: Some Lessons from the Law." In *Negotiating in Organizations*, edited by Max H. Bazerman and Roy J. Lewicki. Beverly Hills, Calif.: Sage, 1983, pp. 193–213.

Sigmon, E. Brent. "Achieving a Negotiated Compensation Agreement in Siting: The MRS Case." *Journal of Policy Analysis and Management* 6 (Winter 1987): 170–79.

Simon, Herbert A. "The Proverbs of Administration." *Public Administration Review* 6 (Winter 1946): 53–67.

Simon, Herbert A. *Administrative Behavior: A Study of Decision-making Processes in Administrative Organization*. New York: Macmillan, 1947.

Simon, Herbert A. *Administrative Behavior*. 3d ed. New York: Free Press, 1976.

Smith, Richard W. "A Theoretical Basis for Participatory Planning." *Policy Sciences* 4 (September 1973): 275–95.

Stanfield, Rochelle L. "Resolving Disputes." *National Journal*, 15 November 1986, pp. 2764–68.

State of New York v. Richard S. Schweiker. 557 F.Supp. 354 (1983).

Stein, Harold, editor. *Public Administration and Policy Development: A Case Book*. New York: Harcourt Brace, 1952.

Stewart, Richard. "The Reformation of American Administrative Law." *Harvard Law Review* 88 (June 1975): 1669–1813.

Stockman, David A. "The Social Pork Barrel." *The Public Interest* (Spring 1975): 3–30.

Stockman, David A. *The Triumph of Politics*. New York: Harper & Row, 1986.

Stone, Deborah A. *Policy Paradox and Political Reason*. Glenview, Ill.: Scott, Foresman, 1988.

Stout, Russell, Jr. *Management or Control? The Organizational Challenge*. Bloomington, Ind.: Indiana University Press, 1980.

Susskind, Lawrence. "Environmental Mediation and the Accountability Problem." *Vermont Law Review* 6 (Spring 1981): 1–47.

Susskind, Lawrence, and Jeffrey Cruikshank. *Breaking the Impasse: Consensual Approaches to Resolving Public Disputes*. New York: Basic Books, 1987.

Szanton, Peter. *Federal Reorganization: What Have We Learned?* Chatham, N.J.: Chatham House, 1981.

Taylor, Frederick Winslow. *The Principles of Scientific Management*. New York: Harper, 1911.

Taylor, Serge. *Making Bureaucracies Think: The Environmental Impact Statement Strategy of Administrative Reform*. Stanford: Stanford University Press, 1984.

Thibaut, John, Laurens Walker, Stephen LaTour, and Pauline Houlden. "Procedural Justice as Fairness." *Stanford Law Review* 26 (June 1974): 1271–90.

Thibaut, John, Laurens Walker, and E. Allen Lind. "Adversary Presentation and Bias in Legal Decisionmaking." *Harvard Law Review* 86 (December 1972): 386–401.

Thompson, Dennis F. *John Stuart Mill and Representative Government*. Princeton, N.J.: Princeton University Press, 1976.

Thompson, Dennis F. *Political Ethics and Public Office*. Cambridge, Mass.: Harvard University Press, 1987.

Thompson, James D. *Organizations in Action*. New York: McGraw-Hill, 1967.

Thompson, James D., and Arthur Tuden. "Strategies, Structures and Processes of Organizational Design." In *Comparative Studies in Administration*, edited by James D. Thompson. Pittsburgh: University of Pittsburgh Press, 1959, pp. 195–216.

Tirole, Jean. "Hierarchies and Bureaucracies: On the Role of Collusion in Organizations." *Journal of Law, Economics and Organization* 2 (Fall 1986): 181–214.

Tocqueville, Alexis de. *Democracy in America*. Two volumes. New York: Vintage Books, 1945.

Trento, Joseph J., with reporting and editing by Susan B. Trento. *Prescription for Disaster: From the Glory of Apollo to the Betrayal of the Shuttle*. New York: Crown, 1987.

United States Presidential Commission on the Space Shuttle *Challenger* Accident. *Report to the President*. Washington, D.C.: U.S. Government Printing Office, 6 June 1986.

Van de Ven, Andrew H. "The Rs of Administrative Behavior: Rationality, Randomness, and Reason (and the Greatest of These Is Reason)." In *Organizational Theory and Public Policy*, edited by Richard H. Hall and Robert E. Quinn. Beverly Hills, Calif.: Sage, 1983, pp. 37–53.

Van de Ven, Andrew H., and Diane L. Ferry. *Measuring and Assessing Organizations*. New York: Wiley, 1980.

Von Bertalanffy, Ludwig. *General Systems Theory: Foundations, Development, Application*. New York: Braziller, 1968.

Walcott, Charles. "Incrementalism and Rationality: An Experimental Study of Budgetary Decision-making." *Experimental Study of Politics* 1 (December 1971): 1–34.

Walcott, Charles, and Karen M. Hult. "Organizing the White House: Structure, Environment, and Organizational Governance." *American Journal of Political Science* 31 (February 1987): 109–25.

Walcott, Charles, and Karen M. Hult. "Management Science and the Great Engineer: Governing the White House during the Hoover Administration." *Presidential Studies Quarterly*, forthcoming.

Waldo, Dwight. "Organization Theory: An Elephantine Problem." *Public Administration Review* 21 (Autumn 1961): 216–21.

Waldo, Dwight. "Organization Theory: Revisiting the Elephant." *Public Administration Review* 38 (November/December 1978): 589–97.

Walker, Wallace Earl. *Changing Organizational Culture: Strategy, Structure, and Professionalism in the U.S. General Accounting Office*. Knoxville, Tenn.: University of Tennessee Press, 1986.

Wamsley, Gary L. "Bureaucratic Governance." Paper presented at the annual meeting of the American Political Science Association, Washington, D.C., 1984.

Warwick, Donald P., in collaboration with Marvin Meade and Theodore Reed. *A Theory of Public Bureaucracy: Politics, Personality, and Organization in the State Department*. Cambridge, Mass.: Harvard University Press, 1975.

Waterman, Richard W. "Reagan and the Environmental Protection Agency: Revolution and Counter-revolution." Paper presented at the annual meeting of the Midwest Political Science Association, Chicago, 1987.

Weber, Max. "Bureaucracy." In *Max Weber: Essays in Sociology*, edited by Hans Gerth and C. Wright Mills. New York: Oxford University Press, 1946, pp. 196–230.

Weinberg, Alvin M. "Science and Trans-science." *Minerva* 10 (April 1979): 209–22.

West, William F. *Administrative Rulemaking: Politics and Processes*. Westport, Conn.: Greenwood Press, 1985.

West, William F. "The Organizational Dynamics of Administrative Regulation: A Preliminary Discussion." Paper presented at the annual meeting of the Western Political Science Association, Anaheim, Calif., 1987.

White, Orion F., Jr. "The Dialectical Organization: An Alternative to Bureaucracy." *Public Administration Review* 29 (January/February 1969): 32–42.

Whiteside, David E. "Roger Smith's Campaign to Change the GM Culture." *Business Week*, 7 April 1986, pp. 84–85.

Whitney, Scott Cameron. "Technical and Scientific Evidence in Administrative Adjudication." *University of Cincinnati Law Review* 45 (Winter 1976): 37–55.

Wholey, Joseph S., Mark A. Abramson, and Christopher Bellavita. *Performance and Credibility: Developing Excellence in Public and Nonprofit Organizations.* Lexington, Mass.: D. C. Heath, 1986.

Williamson, Oliver. "The Economics of Organization: The Transaction Cost Approach." *American Journal of Sociology* 87 (November 1981): 548–77. (a)

Williamson, Oliver E. "Saccharin: An Economist's View." In *The Scientific Basis of Health and Safety Regulation,* edited by Robert W. Crandall and Lester B. Lave. Washington, D.C.: Brookings Institution, 1981, pp. 131–51. (b)

Wilson, Harlan. "Complexity as a Theoretical Problem: Wider Perspectives in Political Theory." In *Organized Social Complexity: Challenge to Politics and Policy,* edited by Todd L. LaPorte. Princeton, N.J.: Princeton University Press, 1975, pp. 281–331.

Wilson, Woodrow. "The Study of Administration." *Political Science Quarterly* 2 (June 1887): 197–222.

Wolff, Robert Paul. *In Defense of Anarchism.* New York: Harper & Row, 1970.

Wood, B. Dan. "Principals, Bureaucrats, and Responsiveness in Clean Air Enforcement." *American Political Science Review* 82 (March 1988): 213–34.

Woodward, Bob. *Veil: The Secret Wars of the CIA, 1981–1987.* New York: Simon and Schuster, 1987.

Yates, Douglas. *Bureaucratic Democracy: The Search for Democracy and Efficiency in American Government.* Cambridge, Mass.: Harvard University Press, 1982.

Yates, Douglas. *The Politics of Management.* San Francisco: Jossey-Bass, 1985.

Yellin, Joel. "High Technology and the Courts: Nuclear Power and the Need for Institutional Reform." *Harvard Law Review* 94 (January 1981): 489–560.

Yellin, Joel. "Science, Technology, and Administrative Government: Institutional Designs for Environmental Decisionmaking." *Yale Law Journal* 92 (June 1983): 1300–33.

Zald, Mayer, and Roberta Ash. "Social Movement Organizations: Growth, Decay, and Change." *Social Forces* 44 (March 1966): 327–41.

Zaleznik, Abraham. "Power and Politics in Organizational Life." *Harvard Business Review* 48 (May/June 1970): 47–60.

Index